The Man Who Mc
A Cathedral

Richard Poore, Dean of Old Sarum 1194 - 1215

Bishop of Winchester 1215 - 17

Bishop of Old Sarum and Salisbury 1217 - 28
(showing a model of his half-completed Cathedral)

Bishop of Durham 1228 - until his death in 1236

Sarum Cathedral in the 12th C

Salisbury Cathedral in the 21st C

William Longespée, 3rd Earl of Salisbury alias Longsword (1167-1226) natural son of King Henry II and Countess Ida, daughter of Earl Richard of Tosni in France (she later married Roger Bigod, 2nd Earl of Norfolk). He is shown lying in peace in Salisbury Cathedral. *See also page 46.*

About the Author

Tim Hatton joined the Indian Army from school in 1943 and was commissioned into the 9th Gurkha Rifles in 1944 serving as a Company Commander in the Far East (Dutch East Indies) and in India during the Partition of the Punjab, where he escorted 100,000 Muslims on foot and in strict purdah through hostile Indian territory to the safety of Pakistan. He was appointed to the Colonial Service in 1948 and took part throughout the Malayan and Malaysian Emergencies retiring in 1966 as Director of Malaysia's Special Branch. He received the MBE and, later, the OBE and the Colonial Police Medal. He was also honoured by the Malayan and Malaysian Governments.

On return to the UK he took the Open Examination for entry into the Home Civil Service and was appointed Principal in HM Treasury. He also became Hon Treasurer of the British Atlantic Committee, soon to become the Atlantic Council of NATO, of which Tim was appointed a member of the President's Advisory Committee.

He was elected a Freeman of the City of London in 1978 and was for many years Chairman of the London Branch of the Voluntary Aided Schools Association and the Director of the United Westminster Schools Foundation and the Royal Foundation of Greycoat Hospital. Both included secondary schools in the state and independent sectors of education. In addition he was Chairman for ten years of the Governing Body of an independent school; Committee Member of the Round Square Conference Group of Schools; a Governor of the Hellenic College of London for six years and is currently Vice-President of the English-Speaking Union Salisbury Branch.

He was recently awarded by HM King Constantine of the Hellenes Honorary Membership of the Round Square Association of Schools in recognition of outstanding service beyond expectation.

He has two sons from his first wife, the late Joanna Tarver; he and his second wife Sarah moved to Salisbury in 1994. Tim has been a Salisbury Cathedral guide and a Friend of Salisbury Cathedral for eighteen years and much enjoys helping foreign tourists so making their visits to the cathedral even more of a memorable occasion! He is a published author (*Tock Tock Birds*, *A Spider in the Web of International Terrorism*, published in the UK and Malaysia) and maintains contacts with friends and associates worldwide.

Author's Note: Every effort has been made to trace the identified copyright holders; but if any have been inadvertently overlooked, the author will be pleased to rectify the matter at the first opportunity.

Published by T. E. Hatton OBE
© Copyright 2012

The text is set in New Baskerville.

Printed by Salisbury Printing Company Limited
Greencroft Street, Salisbury, Wiltshire SP1 1JF Tel: 01722 413330

ISBN 978-0-9574148-0-8

Author's Comments

This book is dedicated to the 600 volunteers who have given, and continue to give, their patience, expertise and a great deal of their time for the benefit of Salisbury Cathedral. Having been a frequent visitor to the Cathedral over eight decades and having the privilege of working as a cathedral guide and having taken part in various other cathedral activities over the last 18 years, I continue to be amazed at the professional proficiency of today's splendid volunteers and their never-failing good humour.

The result is that today's cathedral visitors are well looked after and able to discuss, appreciate and enjoy the wealth of attractions which Salisbury Cathedral has to offer. I salute all the volunteers and admire their achievements.

An interesting point which I think worthwhile noting is that the intention of the 12th C planners under Bishop Hubert Walter – and implemented by that outstanding leader of men Bishop Richard Poore – was not just to build another cathedral to replace the old cramped one where life had become intolerable for those who lived and worked on top of Old Sarum and who suffered immensely from the devious activities of the Norman soldiers. Rather it was a deliberate transfer of religious life, and the worship of God, from Old Sarum to a much quieter place in pleasanter and safer surroundings. In other words, the move was deliberately planned to be a geographical and religious transfer without a break in religious worship ("The King is dead, long live the King" as Tim Tatton Brown, till recently Salisbury Cathedral's Consultant Architect, was prone to say). This intended continuity of worship and the enormous physical building problems and the vast expense involved are not always understood and appreciated today, I think.

I should like to quote a comment by Bishop Nicholas Sarum in a recent issue of the Cathedral Friends' Magazine "The Cathedral is a great architecture, certainly, but it has a transcendent beauty that lifts our hearts to God as well as being a taste of Heaven on earth". How the 12th and 13th century planners and their builders too would have enjoyed and appreciated this inspiring description almost a thousand years 'later'!

I am particularly grateful to my wife, Sarah, who has once again given up so much of her time to the production stages of this book, accompanying me on our expeditions hunting for and gathering material from sources all over England, and also entertaining in our home a most interesting variety of new friends; then transferring all the information gained into little computer sticks for the printing press.

Above all, I am equally indebted to the host of sources whose names appear on the Lists of People and Resources at the back of the book. I am grateful for the practical and friendly help given to us by Steve Hurley, the Commercial Director of Salisbury Printing Ltd – working with him and his efficient and reliable staff has been a most enjoyable experience for both of us.

My special thanks also go to: Dr Pamela Blum, Dr Julia Boorman, Dr Clare Brea, Sarah Brown, The Rev Ben Elliott, Dr Rodney Atwood, Professor Brian Kemp, Roy Spring, Tim Tatton Brown and Major General Roy Dixon who has written for the Cathedral Guides his own excellent updated study of places, objects and people connected with the history of Salisbury Cathedral.

Finally, I hope that readers of this book will find it an interesting handbook of the past which describes the building of Salisbury Cathedral and includes a cross-section of interesting 13th C characters involved – with just a little bit of fun thrown in on the way.

Tim Hatton

List of Chapters

Appendices

Note: Maps illustrating the Middle East Holy Land Pilgrimages and the Crusades from 1096-1254 may be found at both ends of the book.

The Wessex Factor

Saxon invaders are reputed to have selected the word Wessex to describe the centre of their occupation of Western England in about 499AD. Wessex soon expanded into what is now Dorset, Somerset, Wiltshire and Hampshire. The Kings of Wessex were descended from their original founder, Cerdic (r. 519-534) who was succeeded by his son Cynric (r. 534-560) famous for his defeat of the 'Britons' at Old Sarum in 552. After a stream of 22 Kings, Alfred the Great (r. 871-899) ascended the throne. He saved England from a major Danish invasion, laid a base for national unity and promoted learning. He built 30 forts (burghs) and is considered to have founded the Royal Navy. Although a wise ruler who introduced a measure of land reform; he did not suffer fools gladly and achieved his aims by being quite ruthless at times. He visited Rome in 853 and again in 855, becoming a devout Christian and a recognised scholar.

The Peace of Wedmore in 878, which followed King Alfred's military victory at the Battle of Ethandune, near Eddington in Wiltshire, resulted in a treaty between Alfred and the Scandinavian King Guthrum. The Vikings agreed to hand over hostages to Alfred, to leave Wessex altogether and to accept Christianity.

Although Wessex had now effectively been subsumed into the larger kingdom which its expansion had created, like the other former kingdoms it continued for a time to have a distinct identity which periodically found renewed political expression. After the death of King Eadred in 955 England was divided between his two sons, with the elder Edwy ruling in Wessex, while Mercia passed to his younger brother Edgar.

Having occupied much of England in 1016, the Danish King Canute established earldoms based on the four kingdoms of Northumbria, Mercia and East Anglia, but initially he administered Wessex personally. Within a few years, however, he had created an earldom of Wessex, encompassing most of England south of the Thames, for his English henchman Godwin. For almost 50 years the vastly wealthy holders of this earldom, firstly Godwin (1001-53) and then his son Harold, were the most powerful men in English politics after the King. Finally, on the death of Edward the Confessor in 1066, Harold became King Harold II thus reuniting the earldom of Wessex with the Crown of England. But he did not last long for he was killed at the Battle of Hastings (some say he was killed by a sword thrust and not from an arrow in his eye as portrayed in the Bayeaux Tapestry). Following the Norman conquest in 1066 King William I bestowed the earldom of Wessex on William Fitzosbern (c.1020-71). After his death the earldom faded away.

The second and current creation of the Wessex earldom dates from 19th June 1999 when HM Queen Elizabeth II created HRH Prince Edward, her youngest son, Earl of Wessex.

The name Wessex was reintroduced into the English language by the novelist Thomas Hardy (1840-1928) who explained 'finding the area of a single county did not offer (me) a canvas large enough .... and that there were no objections to an invented name, I disinterred the old one'. (quoted from Brewer's Directory of Phrase and Fable).

Like Hardy's widely read novels, Wessex not only provides a lively background to much of our book: but is also a pleasant, friendly place in which to live or visit today.

Chapter One

The Origin and Rise of the Normans in Western Europe. Earl William Longespée's Scandinavian Ancestry. Sarum Castle. The Battle of Hastings 1066. The Systematic Destruction of the English Feudal System and its Complete Replacement by a Strict Norman Administration. The Domesday Survey and Council of Sarum 1087. Bishop (Saint) Osmund. Saint Aldhelm. John of Salisbury. Two Other Famous Norman Bishops. The Move to New Sarum. Wilton Town, Saints Edith and Iwi, and the Monk Goscelin. The Decline and Rebirth of Wilton Town.

> *"(the Norman leaders) were all personally repellent, cruel and coldly unscrupulous. They were men of great ability and vastly ambitious. Endowed with vision, if sometimes restricted, they all pursued their purpose with inflexible determination – above everything, they were masterful and able to deal with the astute and vigorous company of Norman magnates who surrounded them".*
>
> DAVID C DOUGLAS, MODERN HISTORIAN AND AUTHOR

The Origin and Rise of the Normans

During the 9th and 10th centuries piracy raged around the seas of Britain and the coasts of Northern France. As time went by these pirates established settlements on land. The majority came from Scandinavia and the most ferocious of these was called Rolf (later Gallicised as Rollo), a native of Norway. One day, a small fleet of these experienced pirates, led by Rollo, sailed from Scandinavia into the estuary of the river Loire in N W France. They landed and fought their way northeastwards. Here they were intercepted near the Gallic city of Chartres where they were defeated by the superior forces of Emperor Charles III in 911. It seems that the Emperor regarded discretion to be the better part of valour and spared Rollo and his men providing Rollo agreed to become Christian. This he did and was baptised by the Archbishop of Rouen, upon which the Emperor gave Rollo extensive grants of land. Although Rollo eventually returned to paganism, his son William Longespée acquired much more land and great authority over that part of France which, generally, became known as Normandy (i.e. from the Norse 'Normadre' meaning 'North Man').

The History Today Companion to British History notes that the Duchy of Normandy was created in N W France during the 10th century following the Treaty of Saint Claire-sur-Epte arranged between Rollo, the Vikings' Chieftan, and the local Frankish inhabitants. The Vikings soon integrated with the Normans and their combined ventures across the English Channel became a constant source of worry for the Anglo-Saxons. Eventually, in 1066, these Normans under King William the Conqueror defeated the English at the Battle of Hastings and established the House of Normandy on the throne of England.

Brewer's Millennium Edition Directory (p.1000) describes Rollo as a Norman pirate (c. 860-933) who attacked Paris and Chartres and, eventually, secured from Emperor Charles III of France a large district on condition that he baptised and became Charles' vassal. One of his descendants was his great great grandchild William, Duke of Normandy and Conqueror of England, who himself, was the great grandfather of Earl William Longespée.

Elsie Rousedahl, editor of the book *'From Viking to Crusader, Scandinavians in Europe 800-1200 AD' (pub. Rizzoli 1992)*, notes that a Scandinavian called William Longespée, son of Rollo, established himself in Rouen, France c. 919. He gave endowments to monks and married a Carolingan princess.

William the Conqueror lands on England 1066 from *The Comic History of England* by G A A Beckett, illustrated by John Leech, published by Routledge c. 1850.

The Norman hierarchy were great travellers both by circumstance and choice. It soon came to pass that they invaded countries and states such as England, northern and central France, Southern Italy as far north as the outskirts of Rome, and Sicily. Their tentacles reached out along the coastline of the Mediterranean including Antioch and Latakia in Northern Palestine where they set up a Principality c. 1100. In addition to conquering these areas they interfered in the affairs of the Byzantine (Eastern Empire) and the Seljuk (Turkish) Empire. Their conquests were often facilitated by use of the self-styled claim that they were 'soldiers of Christ'.

It is interesting and relevant to our story to discover something about the Norman leaders' characters, especially what drove such a small nation and how they were able to change the course of European history to such an amazing extent. David C. Douglas, historian and recent author of *'The Normans'* has studied these matters at length and has summarised his views on the Norman character as follows 'the greatest of the early Norman leaders from

The Bayeux Tapestry – Bishop Odo urges on the Norman Cavalry.

1000 to 1150 was William the Conqueror, bastard son of Robert I, Duke of Normandy, (d. 1035), and his paramour Herleve, daughter of Fulbert, a tanner from Falaise. Norman leaders were not thick on the ground nor were their armies, but they managed to dominate most of Europe and part of the Middle East for over 150 years. Douglas has very strong words to define the Norman character – *see Page 7 in italics*. Incidentally, he notes that William the Conqueror was the fifth descendant of Rollo the Pirate.

David Douglas, in his Epilogue to *'The Normans'*, considers the Norman contribution to the history of Europe between 1100-1154 to have been a permanent performance and of particular (historic) interest. It was made during the years when Latin

'The Coronation of William the Conqueror (r. 1066-1087)'.
By kind permission of the British Library.

Christianity was attaining a new sense of political unity which would, in its turn, promote the formation of European identity. In this process the Normans were intimately involved e.g. the practical after-effects of Norman government in England were positive and long lasting. By 1154, the defeat or replacement of Norman controlled governments in England, Sicily and the Eastern Mediterranean did not mean that the Norman occupiers of these countries, perforce or otherwise, fled back to their homeland. Rather the reverse, the Normans stayed on, having married local girls and produced families generation after generation.

Sarum Castle – The Norman Soldiers Move In

The castle site on the hill at Old Sarum had been inhabited over many centuries and was the scene of much fighting and was often used as a place of refuge. The hill was called Sorviodunum (dunum is the Celtic for hill fort) in Celtic/Roman times; Sarisberie, Sarisberie or Sarisburh by the Anglo-Saxons and then the Normans (bury, berie and burg are the Anglo-Saxon/Norman words for a fortified town) – all with some variations. It became Old Sarum in late medieval times.

The castle was built in the 11th century by the Normans, shortly after the battle of Hastings in 1066, as part of William the Conqueror's drive to turn England into a Norman State. It was built on a chalky hill site in a good defensive position inside Iron Age earthworks, with a motte and castle at its centre. After further substantial improvements to the fortifications it became a Royal Castle under command of a castellan appointed by the king. The site was conveniently close to the town of Wilton where there was an important abbey and a royal nunnery.

William Cobbett (1763-1835), politician and writer, described in his forthright manner 'Old Sarum may be compared with three cheeses, one on top of the other – the broadest at the bottom, and the top one looking like a Stilton'. John Chadwick, author, says that John Constable's watercolour viewed from the south catches this impression. Samuel Pepys, the diarist, remarked that it would afright him to be left there at night.

The Domesday Survey

In 1085 the aged King William Conqueror of England, tired of defending his newly won kingdom of England against military incursions from France (Flanders) and Scandinavia, decided to strengthen his political hold on England by the introduction of an entirely new feudal system which would ensure civil stability, Norman political power and his military strength. So he introduced an extensive Survey of the land in England (excluding London, Winchester, and the four northern counties) in order to provide him with an informed basis for Norman rule and taxation of the inhabitants. It was the most extensive survey carried out in medieval times. But it caused considerable discontent among the Anglo-Saxons. It was a revolutionary change resulting in the final collapse of Anglo-Saxon power and its replacement by a new and very powerful Norman aristocracy.

According to John Morris, the General Editor of 'Domesday 6 Wiltshire' published by Phillimore of Chichester in 1979, King William the Conqueror instructed his Commissioners to send men all over England to each shire ... to find out ... what or how much each landholder held ... in land and livestock and what it was worth. The results were to be brought back to him personally. Later on, a second set of Commissioners were sent to the shires, which they did not know and where they themselves were unknown, to check their predecessors' survey and report any discrepancies back to the king.

The Commissioners' brief included:

> The name of the place visited. Who held it before 1066 and now.
>
> The number of hides. How many ploughs, both those in lordship and those belonging to their men.
>
> The number of villagers, cottagers and slaves. And the number of free men.
>
> The amount of woodlands, meadows, and pastures. The number of mills and fishponds.
>
> Details of any additions or removals since the previous survey.
>
> The total value before and after the visits; and the total amount possessed by every free man or Freeman has or had before 1066.

NB. A hide is defined by the Shorter Oxford English Dictionary (SOED) as a measure of land in Anglo-Saxon and early Norman times and especially to estimate the amount of land needed to support one family and varied in extent from 60 to 120 acres according to locality.

Thus all the land belonged to the King as the Lord Paramount and was divided into fiefs – 60,215 of them. Vassals of the King undertook to conscript men for his army to serve up to forty days in the year: and the King could rely on the supply of money to pay for a large army at short notice in an emergency.

The use of the word Domesday (as in Survey or Book) is a reflection of the anger and despair of the Anglo-Saxon community throughout England when the effect of the Survey became only too clear to them. The dispossession of much of their lands and properties was a 'done deal' without any appeal, similar to the Last Day of Judgement or Doom's Day. The Domesday Book itself is now in the Public Records Office in Kew, Richmond, London.

The Council of Sarum

On 1st August 1086 King William convoked a great Witangemut (Anglo-Saxon word for a gathering of wise men) in the castle's precincts. Here he received the fealities of a multitude of barons, bishops, major landowners and wealthy merchants from all round England. Those present took a formal oath of loyalty to the king (the famous Oath of Sarum) then the King formally accepted the Domesday Survey. Eventually, however, the events on 1st August 1066 provided the basis of uniting the Norman and English into one nation.

Bishop Herman (1075-78) Starts Building Sarum Cathedral next to the Castle

Soon after the Norman soldiers moved into the castle decisions were taken at the Council of London, in 1075, which decreed that bishoprics should be based not in villages or small towns but in larger and more important settlements. Consequently, Bishop Herman, or Hereman, originally from Lorraine, a monastic bishop, was translated from the combined Sees of Ramsbury and Sherborne to Sarum in 1075. He set about building a new cathedral beside the recently completed castle on top of the hill. He died three years later on 20 February 1078 and was succeeded by Bishop Osmund, a secular bishop.

An aerial photograph of the remains of Old Sarum Cathedral is on page 19.

Bishop Osmund

Professor Diana Greenway FBA Medieval History and Paleography and author, notes 'little is known of Bishop Osmund's family and background in France, other than he was probably a younger son of a member of the Norman ruling class. He became a learned scholar and was a much trusted senior official in King William I's court and served as Royal Chancellor of England from 1070-78. He, and his canons, carried out a great deal of work on the composition of the Doomsday Book'. He became personally involved with the construction of the new cathedral beside the castle on Sarum Hill. Its foundation charter of 1091 was sealed by King William 11 (Rufus) and its opening paragraph reads 'In the name of the holy and undivided Trinity, I, Osmund, Bishop of the Church of Sarum, make known to all Christ's faithful people, present and future, that I have built the Church of Sarum in honour of our Lord Jesus Christ and the most Holy Virgin Mary and for the help of the souls of King William and his wife Matilda and his son William, King of the English, successor of the realm, and also for the health of my own soul; and I have established canons therein, and have granted them, while they live according to rule, church property in perpetuity as I myself obtained it'. Five days after the consecration of his cathedral on 5 April 1092 the central tower was struck by lightning during a storm. It caught fire and collapsed and had to be re-built. Osmund was the most popular of the early excellent Norman bishops of Sarum and seems to have gone out of his way to learn the Anglo-Saxon language and to understand the plight of the defeated English. He gave substantial sums of money and gifts of land to finance the building of his cathedral, he founded Sarum Cathedral Boys' Choir School for both Norman and Anglo-Saxon boys in 1091, and took a personal interest in their further education.

Bishop Osmund's Choir School for Boys in Sarum and later, in Salisbury

Professor Nicholas Orme, of Exeter University, historian, reminds us that 'for a long time after the foundation of Osmund's choir school, the boys spent a great deal of their time carrying out menial duties in and around the church as well as taking part in the services. As they became experienced and useful in carrying out these duties they developed into a valuable source of recruitment for the adult clergy'. In 1991 the Cathedral authorities decided to celebrate their nine hundredth anniversary by admitting girls into their choir school. Thus Salisbury was the first cathedral in England to establish a girls' choir school alongside, but separate from, its boys' choir school; their voices being trained separately but enjoying academic teaching in mixed classes. Both choirs have since become internationally famous. Perhaps the greatest local 'old boy' of those early days was John of Salisbury, Bishop of Chartres in France, who was regarded, in his lifetime, as a great humanist, a cultured man and an outstanding leader of the literary renaissance of the 12th Century. *See also pp 14-17, 49.*

Bishop Osmund was an acknowledged scholar and amassed a great collection of documents and books, he seems to have bound many of the latter. He founded what became one of the most famous libraries in the land. Much of his work and his library survive today creating a wonderful source for research by medieval scholars.

Salisbury Cathedral authorities' interest in the basic education of young boys, apart from its choir school, continued after the cathedral moved from Sarum to New Sarum. In 1260 Bishop Giles de Bridport founded the College of De Vaux in the southern end of the Close, near the Avon River, opposite the Hospital of St Nicholas (founded 1215).

Recently, Professor Nicholas Orme has noted 'the cathedral authorities (in the early days) managed a fee-paying grammar school for the town and the diocese which was located in the Old High Street, near Exeter Street opposite St Ann Gate.

For further information of De Vaux College and St Nicholas Hospital, please see Appendix II, pages 112-124.

Bishop St Osmund's effigy in St Peter's Basilica, Rome.

Bishop Osmund dies 1099

After his death, during the night of 3/4 December 1099 at the age of about fifty nine, Diana Greenway says that he was buried in a place of honour in the choir of his Cathedral. Later on his tomb was moved to a special place in the east end of the enlarged cathedral. On Trinity Sunday the 14th June 1226, Bishop Osmund's tomb and the tombs of his successors, Bishops Roger and Jocelin, were brought down from Sarum Hill and laid to rest in the almost completed Trinity Chapel at the east end of Salisbury Cathedral.

Bishop Osmund is Canonised in 1457

Efforts were made to persuade succeeding Popes to canonise him; but, for various reasons, to no avail until 1 January 1457 when Bishop Richard Beauchamp, having taken a personal interest, persuaded Pope Calixtus III to approve Osmund's canonisation. The Pope issued a mandate to the Bishop authorising him to prepare a shrine and translate the relics. Thus, at last, work could start on the building of his shrine in its lovingly reserved place in the Trinity Chapel at the east end of Salisbury Cathedral. Pilgrims soon came from far and wide. Sadly, some eighty two years later, shrines were abolished during the Reformation and, in 1539, Saint Osmund's shrine was dismantled over a period of fifty two man-days, taken to London and sold for today's equivalent of a few million pounds.

All that is left today is a carved black Tournai marble tomb slab now resting upon the original position of the shrine; and part of the saint's Purbeck marble (shelly limestone) tomb distinguished by six foramina (holes or openings) into which sick people could place their diseased limbs as near as possible to the saint's body below in the hope of a

Bishop St Osmund's tomb in Salisbury Cathedral.

miraculous recovery. Roy Spring, Salisbury Cathedral's Clerk of Works, now retired, notes that 'for a long period from the 16th to the 19th centuries this tomb was described as being that of Lord Charles Stourton (who, in 1556, was hanged in Salisbury marketplace for killing Mr Hartgill and his son)'. This was during the time of the Reformation and its re-use by the Stourton family may well be true. Spring goes on to suggest that 'the re-used tomb might have been placed within the doorway of the original Beauchamp chapel (later destroyed by James Wyatt, the architect, c. 1790) and within the thickness of the cathedral wall – a fitting place for the body of a murderer – neither within nor without consecrated ground'. Thus, perhaps, this tomb was indeed part of St Osmund's shrine and has returned to its rightful home in the Trinity Chapel, now sometimes known as the Prisoners of Conscience chapel. Sadly, St Osmund's remains have long since disappeared (probably when the tomb was desecrated in the Reformation). His statue may be seen on the west front of Salisbury Cathedral holding his books.

At or near his tomb, a number of witnessed miracles (as defined medically over 800 years ago) were carefully recorded. Professor Nicholas Orme notes that, of these, three miracles attributed to St Osmund involved the miraculous recovery of John Westmore, a two year old boy who had fallen into a stream; Christine Cerlee, aged nine, who had been struck on the head by an iron quoit; and Agnes Bromley, aged fourteen, who had been wounded by a spit. All three made pilgrimages to St Osmund's shrine with their families after their recovery and Christine's quoit was offered at the shrine.

The earliest miracles at this tomb were written down by 1218 when a dossier was being put together in support of the first application to Rome for Osmund's canonisation. One of the Salisbury witnesses said he knew of more than a hundred cures of toothache that had occurred at Osmund's tomb, and that the tomb itself must have had a special power, for a man with a diseased jaw-bone was healed while rubbing it on the stonework. Another man, who carelessly sat on the tomb, was immediately struck by a severe pain in the head which made him feel as if his eyes were falling out; he went home but was in such agony he could not eat. A friend asked him when he first felt the pain and, on hearing that the man was sitting on Osmund's tomb at the time, he cried out in horror and told him to go back quickly to beg the saint's forgiveness. This the man did, with tears and prayers – and he was cured.

Osmund was one of only a dozen English saints to be canonised by a Pope before the Reformation of the 1530s. He was also the last. In the crypt of St Peter's Basilica in Rome, beside the tomb of Pope Calixtus III, there is a fine relief sculpture, dating from shortly after the canonisation, showing Osmund in his episcopal vestments and carrying the model of a cathedral (Sarum), signifying his role as its founder. Diana Greenway comments 'the existence of the sculpture is a sign of the esteem in which Salisbury's saint was regarded in Rome itself, the command centre of the Western Church'. *(Please see photograph on page 12)*

The Miniature Lives of the Saints, published by Burns and Oates, has these notes on St Osmund and St Anselm (not to be confused with the earlier St Aldhelm)

'Being in everything zealous for the glory of God's house Bishop Osmund finished the building of his predecessor's cathedral at Old Sarum giving it a chapter of canons and a school'. Osmund seems to have been of a retiring disposition, fonder of copying and binding books than of the public affairs in which he had to take part. At the Council of Rockingham in 1095 he was induced to join those who, to please King William II, opposed St Anselm, Archbishop of Canterbury; but later saw his mistake, and asked Anselm's forgiveness for his opposition. Osmund was known for his strictness with penitents and was no less strict in his own life. His canonisation was the last to take place in England until 1935. His feast day is kept on December 4th'.

Saint Aldhelm, Bishop Osmund's Role-Model (c. 639-709)
Anglo-Saxon Saint and Bishop of Sherborne

The dire results of the full-scale Norman invasion of England in 1066 must have deeply affected Osmund's feelings – the contemporary Bayeux tapestry at Caen in France illustrates vividly the atrocities committed by the Norman, French and Breton soldiers following the defeat of the English in 1066. William of Poitiers describes the looting of English churches and the chronicler Ordevic Vitalis also describes how the Norman soldiers raped, pillaged and murdered the English. Bishop Osmund would have known all this and he reacted publicly by adopting the Anglo-Saxon Saint Aldhelm as his ideal.

Diana Greenway notes that Aldhelm was the first native Englishman to leave a quantity of work written in Latin and was an immensely learned scholar. He had studied under Theodore, Archbishop of Canterbury (who was a Greek) and Abbot Hadrian, a North African educated in the bi-lingual Greek-Latin community at Naples.

After training, Aldhelm became Abbot of Malmesbury and then the first Bishop of Sherborne (705-9). After his death on 25 May 709 he was buried at Malmesbury.

Diana Greenway notes again that his written works included the well-known book 'On Virginity' of which there is a precious manuscript copy, acquired in the time of St Osmund, and still preserved in the library of Salisbury Cathedral (MS 38).

It is significant of Osmund's devotion to Aldhelm that his first recorded act, after becoming bishop, was to preside on 3rd June 1078 at a service in Malmesbury Abbey during which Aldhelm's remains were taken with great reverence from their resting place and enclosed in a new casket or shrine. Soon afterwards, Osmund requested a relic of St. Aldhelm from the Abbot of Malmesbury, and was given a piece of bone from the saint's left arm which he put in a costly and beautifully crafted silver box to be kept in the cathedral at Old Sarum. It is listed in an inventory of that cathedral's treasures, drawn up in 1214, as 'the arm of St Aldhelm covered in silver, with many stones' (it has since disappeared – probably during the Reformation).

As William of Malmesbury records, Osmund was anxious to demonstrate the continuity of the episcopal see. Aldhelm was the first bishop and founder of the see at Sherborne; Osmund was the first bishop to be consecrated at Sarum.

Author's Note: Bishop (Saint) Aldhelm's statue, recently modelled by Jason Battle, now graces the western front of Salisbury Cathedral.

John of Salisbury (c. 1115-1180), Bishop of Chartres 1176-1180

John of Salisbury favoured the simple title of his native town. Although he died as Bishop of Chartres and was buried in the chapel of St Mary in a monastery near his cathedral, it is by his English birthplace that he is known to posterity.

The future prince of the Church, diplomat and man of letters was born of humble parentage in Old Sarum sometime between 1115-1220. It is not known for certain whether he was of Saxon or Norman origin, nor is his patronymic recorded. However some historians consider that John would almost certainly have considered himself an Englishman. One chronicler refers to him as Johannes Parvus, the Little, reflecting his stature rather than his origins. Old Sarum, at that time, was a city divided against itself. The conflict between the noblemen and their soldiers, and the clerics and their families during this period of English history was particularly bitter within the moated confines which, perforce, they had to share. John would have been only too aware of this difficult situation.

Bishop St Osmund had founded a choir and grammar school in the city and had formed a fine library for his scholars. John would have become a pupil in this school and attracted the patronage of the local bishop, the autocratic Roger. Thus, from boyhood, John was familiar with the competition for power and preferment, between Crown and Church, which was to involve him in later life when he became an influential advisor to Archbishop Thomas Becket.

The monks of Old Sarum had probably taught their brilliant pupil all they could when, in 1136, John left home in order to continue his studies in Paris. It was an opportune moment for this young man, who throughout his life displayed a talent for avoiding trouble, to leave a country rent by civil war. Old Sarum was deeply involved in the dispute between King Stephen and Matilda over succession to the throne following the death of Henry I in 1135. This soon developed into a state of anarchy. Bishop Roger, John of Salisbury's patron, actively supported Matilda, who eventually became the loser; and Bishop Roger was disgraced, evicted from his See, imprisoned and soon died "more from mortification than old age".

John's knowledge of Roman law and ecclesiastical administration, combined with an outstanding literary talent, earned his entrée to the Papal court. In Rome he developed considerable skill as a diplomat and he claimed that, by 1159, he had crossed the Alps ten times on various missions. John eventually became the confidant and emissary of Cardinal Nicholas Breakespeare, the only English Pope (Adrian IV c. 1100-59), who later entrusted him with the Papal Bull (Seal), and the emerald ring that accompanied it. (Pope Adrian IV later authorised Henry II's invasion of Ireland). In 1148 John joined the household of Archbishop Theobald of Canterbury, to whom he had been introduced during a meeting of the Second Lateran Council in 1139, on the recommendation of St Bernard, Abbot of Clairvaux. Six years later he was appointed the Archbishop's Secretary and played a significant part in the long and bitter disputes between his beloved Archbishop and King Henry II.

Writing some years later, John described France as "the most gentle and civil of all nations". In Paris he studied under some of the finest teachers of the day, including Pierre (Peter) Abelard, and he spent three years as a student in Chartres, at that time the headquarters of what could be called a contemporary humanist movement. In the twenty years following his departure from home John's scholarship and reputation flowered.

During this period a friendship developed between John and another member of the Canterbury clique, Thomas Becket, who had entered the household as a clerk some years earlier. In 1159 John dedicated his two great works, *Metalogicon* and the *Polieraticus* to Becket, who by then, had become Chancellor to Henry II and was accompanying the English King on his war in France. When Thomas succeeded Theobald as Archbishop in 1162 John remained at Canterbury as Becket's loyal friend and trusted counsellor.

Once John had become involved in church politics he seems to have made only occasional visits to his childhood home. Reference to Saresberia are rare in the many letters he wrote throughout his later life. However, in one letter, written to Becket, he mentioned that he gave "the French King greetings from his daughter whom I had seen lately at Salisbury", and in others he wrote at length about a dispute that had arisen in the Salisbury deanery.The Great Council of Barons and Bishops, held at Clarendon Palace in the forests four miles from Old Sarum in 1164, did not afford John an opportunity for one of these rare visits. Sadly, he was banished by King Henry II before the start of the council meeting on account of his known partisanship and in order to deprive Becket of the benefits of his advice.

The Constitutions drawn up at Clarendon were intended to resolve the dispute over the jurisdiction of lay and clerical courts and seemed to arrive at a reasonable compromise.

Becket, after temporary acquiescence to the limitation of Church powers, withdrew his support and also went into exile in France.

John joined Archbishop Becket when he withdrew to Sens, then a most important ecclesiastical centre in France, to escape the king's displeasure. During this period he wrote and published a number of well-received books, including several volumes of his Historia Policraticus (Pontificalis), distinguished by their cultural style and delightful descriptions of Rome – full of anecdotes and vignettes of life in that beautiful city. He amassed an extensive library of books in Latin and he translated many others from Greek into Latin.

When John returned to England in 1170 he wrote a letter to a friend: "I speedily made a visit to my mother, who had been ill these two years, and can joyfully await the day of the Lord now that she has seen me". His mother, of whom he had always written with affection, was no longer living in Salisbury but in Exeter, where John's brother, Richard, held an appointment. It is thought that she died soon after this visit. John then preceded Becket to Canterbury and was in the cathedral on the December day which marked the climax of the quarrel between King and Archbishop. Although John withdrew into the background when Becket confronted his four assassins, he lost no time in writing a vivid, apparently eye-witness, account of the event. In a letter written perhaps only a few days after Thomas's death, he gives the earliest description of the martyrdom. John related that the knights "used their evil swords, when he (Thomas) was dead, to spill his brain and cruelly scatter it, mixed with blood and bones, over the pavement".

John remained in England for nearly six years following Becket's death. He witnessed not only the rapid growth of the martyr's cult; but also many of the miracles that led to the process for Becket's canonisation which was completed within three years. Both contemporary and modern historians have lamented that John's biography of the Saint was both brief and reticent. He also wrote a great deal on political and social matters deploring the decadence of 12th century manners and the ethical lowness of Royalty. His favourite author was Cicero for whom he had great admiration and on whose style he based his own. The quotation ('O tempore. O mores') could, perhaps, have been on John of Salisbury's lips from time to time.

In the summer of 1176 John of Salisbury was elected Bishop of Chartres. During these last years of his life he acted as an intermediary between Henry II and Louis VII and was present as witness when the two kings, to whom he owed allegiance, concluded a peace in September 1177. Under this treaty the two monarchs agreed to go together on a Crusade to the Holy Land but it was a promise they never fulfilled.

John's writings are remarkable for their clarity and vivid description of politics and theology and were received with acclaim among educated colleagues of the 12th century in Western Europe. He has often been described as a great humanist, a cultured man and an outstanding leader of the literary renaissance of the 12th century.

John never knew either of the great churches which now dominate the cities where he was born and ended his days. The present cathedral at Chartres was built after the fire of 1194 destroyed all but the west front of John's cathedral.

The foundation stones of Salisbury Cathedral were laid in the 'rich champagne fields of the Avon Valley' just forty years after John's death.

Author's Notes: According to *Brewer's Directory of Phrase and Fable (millennium edition)*, there were five ecumenical Lateran Councils held in the Church of St John Lateran of Rome in 1123, 39, 79, 1215 and 1512-17. This book refers mainly to the Fourth Lateran Council called by Pope Innocent III to define Catholic Doctrine. The word Lateran comes from the name of the ancient palace of the Lateran family which, later, was used as the official palace of the Popes until their departure to Avignon in 1309. Legend has it that the word Lateran derives from the Latin latere (to hide) and the Latin word rana (frog). Apparently, Emperor Nero once vomited a frog covered with blood which he believed was his own progeny and so he hid it in a vault. The subsequent palace built on the site was called The Lateran or The Palace of the Hidden Frog. It is now a museum.

When John of Salisbury died he left his vestments and his belongings to the cathedral authorities including a phial containing St Thomas Becket's blood.

I am most grateful to June Rockett (journalist, author and historian) for letting me have access to her research on this extraordinarily gifted Son of Salisbury

Succeeding Bishops of Sarum

Roger of Caen followed Bishop Osmund. He was said to have been a humble priest before he caught the eye of King Henry I who appointed him to his court. Roger flourished and rose to become Chancellor and Justiciar before he was appointed to the important See of Sarum in 1102. There was a gap of a further five years before he was formally consecrated in 1107. He set about enlarging and improving the cathedral and acted as Regent of England in the absence of the King who was fighting the French in Normandy. Although he already possessed castles at Devizes, Sherborne and Malmesbury he decided to strengthen his military position by agreeing to become the castellan of Sarum castle too. However, he supported the Empress Matilda in the early days of the Anarchy, which displeased King Stephen (1135-54) who deposed Roger in 1139 and dispossessed him of all his properties. Bishop Roger died in poverty soon after, a broken man; but still popular with his 'flock'.

When King Stephen deposed Bishop Roger the responsibility for Sarum castle reverted to the king. After a gap of three years Bishop Roger was succeeded by another excellent bishop, Jocelin de Bohun (usually pronounced Boon), whose episcopacy lasted from 1142-84. He was succeeded, in turn, by Bishop Hubert Walter, who was appointed by King Richard I (the Lionheart) in 1189; but, after four years (much of which he spent on the 3rd Crusade in the Middle East as Chief of Staff to King Richard), he was translated to the See of Canterbury and soon acted as Regent and Chancellor of England during the king's absences abroad. He was followed by Herbert Poore in 1194 and then by Richard Poore, his half-brother, in 1217, until Richard's translation to the bishopric of Durham in 1228 (in ancient manuscripts the family name of Poore, used in this book, is often written as le Poore or le Poer).

Bishop Osmund's Black Tomb Slab and Shrine

It is very likely that the Tournai marble tomb slab, now resting in the centre of the Trinity Chapel where his shrine used to be, is that of the Blessed Osmund. However, the inscribed date on the slab was said by Colonel Symonds, who visited the cathedral in 1644, to have been newly cut. H de S. Shortt FSA, in his monograph of 1959, says 'since the end of the Middle Ages there has never been any doubt as to the attribution of the slab to St Osmund, and (today) there can be no reasonable doubt about it'.

Bishop Roger's tomb slab,
Salisbury Cathedral c. 1139.

Bishop Roger's Tomb Slab

Shortt says that this tomb slab may be that of Bishop Roger and he supports his attribution by quoting art and design details, of which there are many to be observed; they are typical of many other designs of the same date. Shortt continues 'the carving is in very low relief and the bishop appears to lie in a shallow coffin. His original head cannot have been mitred, but this has been replaced in the 14th century or thereabouts, by a mitred head in Purbeck marble, the arch has been cut to make room for it.

Bishop Jocelin's Tomb Slab

Shortt notes 'this slab is of great interest in the history of English art. The effigy is carved in high relief out of Purbeck marble and is probably the first (accurate) English portrait of a prelate to be placed on his own tomb'. William Dodsworth in the 19th century notes 'the similarity of the figure on the slab to that shown on Jocelin's seal and the style and arrangements of the vestments also show a remarkable likeness. The bishop wears an unusually tall mitre but it is the inscriptions on this tomb which add so much to its interest. On the vertical edge of the tomb is a long epitaph which Shortt translates from the Latin as follows:

> 'They weep today down Salisbury way, for now lieth broken
> Justice's sword, Sarum's bishop and lord, yet low be it spoken,
> While yet alive, the poor used to thrive – he feared not the strong ones
> But was a mace that could batter the face of the proud and the wrong ones.
> Princes in hoards, dukes, nobles and lords as his sires he could muster,
> Bishops were three who had sat in this see, and to them he gave lustre'

Shortt goes on to say that some historians may claim that this epitaph refers to Osmund (probably partly based on a mistranslation of the above) but, in his opinion, this is unlikely. The last line of this quotation is important in this context.

Professor Brian Kemp of Reading University notes 'Salisbury Cathedral has two of the oldest identified episcopal effigies in England. They are of Bishop Roger (died 1139) and Bishop Jocelyn de Bohun (died 1186). Salisbury Cathedral also has the second oldest surviving canopied monument, that of Bishop Giles de Bridport (died 1262)'; and he states further:

> 'The earliest English grave slabs date from the 11th century and, when introduced, were low on the ground, unobtrusive and simple. Later on, the carvings were similar to those of Bishop Roger and Bishop Jocelyn above, they were carved in low relief out of the original slab in a comparatively primitive style. As time went by, (burial) carvings gradually rose out of the slabs into high relief as shown in the effigy of Bishop Bingham (died 1246). The canopy of Bishop Giles de Bridport is in the vanguard of monumental design in England. Salisbury Cathedral's masons, designers and sculptors acquired a great reputation in the early middle ages from their work in Purbeck marble and all their early splendid examples of episcopal and military monuments.'

Where to Go?

No one doubted the need for the civilians to move away from the top of Old Sarum and it was equally obvious that several sites would have been proposed by interested parties. Many subsequent myths exist of which one amusing, and often quoted, is as follows:

'No agreement about a new site was reached. So they asked the castellan of the castle to arrange for an archer to fire an arrow into the air from the top of the highest tower on the castle's outer wall which, when it landed, would mark the place to start building the new cathedral. Off went the archer and climbed the tower; and away sped the arrow into the clouds. Watchers down below clapped their hands and cheered as the arrow disappeared from sight. The children ran after it. But the arrow could not be found. Word was that the archer must have been an English bowman who had used the English secret weapon (i.e. a bow made of very hard yew wood which had a longer range and greater penetration than the French bow made of softer wood). Moreover, they assumed the bowman would have had a flagon of English Strongbow cider to give him strength, and not as was the Norman custom, a draught of imported French vin ordinaire (perhaps, also, the reason why the English outfought the French successfully for the next hundred and fifty years before the French discovered the reason for their defeats). Eventually the arrow was located sticking out of a dead deer in a meadow some two and a half miles away owned by the Poore family. Some Salisbury Cathedral Guides enjoy recounting these legends to interested visitors and conclude by pointing out the place where the deer died 'on the grass beneath the floor', they say 'just where you are sitting'.

Remains of Castle and Cathedral on top of Old Sarum Hill today.

Of course, the obvious place to develop a site on which to build a new cathedral would have been at nearby Wilton, where there was an Abbey and a royal nunnery. But the problem here was said to have been the Holy Abbess, who was a very strong character and would, almost certainly, have clashed with the incoming bishops i.e. the half-brothers Herbert and Richard Poore who held equally strong views. The 'problem' was satisfactorily resolved when the two prelates declared they would give a large part of their land at Merryfield (Myrfield) on which to build the new cathedral. So that was that.

Following the cathedral's move to New Sarum, the castle and the occupied hill soon declined in importance. In c1331 the Pope and King Edward III allowed the stones on the site to be taken away and many were re-erected as a wall round the Close. The original masons' marks may still be detected on many of these stones. *(See photograph of a typical mason's mark on page 118)*

Meanwhile Old Sarum continued its decline until it became one of the 56 rotten boroughs abolished in the Reform Bill of 1832 because its two Members returned to Parliament represented only an uninhabited green mound. It is now maintained by English Heritage.

Today, Old Sarum hill is as rainy and windswept as ever; but flowers and birds abound. Moreover, on a fine day, there are beautiful views to be discovered of Salisbury Cathedral's English Gothic spire as it rises elegantly some 404 feet (123 metres) into the heavens above.

Wilton Town

In early medieval times, Wilton town was of great importance because of its Benedictine Abbey, founded sometime before 934 when King Athelstan (r. 924-939) granted land to the Monastery of St Mary which was one of the great religious foundations of England. Its convent was a house for nuns of royal and aristocratic birth, among whom was Edith, the daughter of King Edgar (959-973).

Wilton town became a borough with an important local mint, one of the earliest in the country, and the borough soon became a trading centre and market. It was probably fortified by King Alfred c. 871. In 1003 the town was destroyed by King Sweyn, originally from Denmark, after Ethelred the Unready murdered many of its Danish settlers. Subsequently the town was rebuilt and recovered its prosperity. It was considered to be of great value when the Domesday Book was completed in 1086. By 1121 the abbey was a royal manor holding several other manors in the county. In the same year King Henry I granted the burgesses their first Charter giving them the right to tolls and dues.

On 1st July 1143, while King Stephen's soldiers were busy refortifying the town, they were surprised by a detachment of Empress Matilda's army under Robert of Gloucester. The latter set fire to the town and the abbey. The abbey was soon rebuilt in stone and in 1154 Henry 11 confirmed the original Charter for the town. A later Charter from King John in 1204 cost the burgesses 100 marks (around £66) and 700 ells (875 yards) of linen cloth. Today the medieval street plan of Wilton is virtually unchanged.

Unfortunately for the habitants of Wilton, the move of the nearby cathedral from Sarum to Salisbury; the construction of the new city of Salisbury; the abandonment of the royal castle, together with the construction of a bridge over the river Avon at Salisbury to provide a direct route to the south coast ports, was a serious blow to Wilton's communications.

However, its main attraction today is Wilton House, a member of the Historic Houses Association and is the beautiful home of the Earl and Countess of Pembroke and their family. Other places for the visitor to explore are the revived carpet business, a purpose-built shopping area and a delightful Victorian Italianate Church built by the architects Thomas Henry Wyatt and David Brandon from 1842-47. Among the architectural pleasures in the church are several interesting 12th and 13th century panels of French medieval stained glass to discover in the fenestration.

Saint Edith (961-984)

Edith was born at Kemsing in Kent, the illegitimate daughter of Edgar the Great and Peaceable, King of all England from 959-975, and Wulfthryth, his concubine, then a novice in the royal convent at Wilton. King Edgar, together with St Dunstan the Archbishop of Canterbury, promoted England's monastic revival; and doubled the realm's mints to sixty. He is celebrated in a stained glass window in Bath Abbey where he consented to be crowned in 973. Shortly after his coronation it is said that his barge was rowed along the River Dee at Chester by eight kings (most were probably of Welsh or Scottish descent). He was buried at Glastonbury, Somerset.

Edith was brought up in Wilton convent and her education was undertaken by Radbod of Rheims and Benno of Treves. She was familiar with life at court and would have been greatly affected by her father's support for the Church and for Saint Dunstan (Archbishop of Canterbury from 961 – 988), who was busy reforming monastic life and creating monasteries, nunneries and monastic schools. Despite her father's entreaties, Edith declined to enter royal society preferring to busy herself within the obscurity of the cloister. Although nominated Abbess of Winchester, Barking and Amesbury she appointed superiors and remained with her mother who had now become Abbess of Wilton (she seems to have made ample amends for her irregularity with King Edgar). After the treacherous murder in 974 of her half-brother, the thirteen year old King Edward (Saint and Martyr) at Corfe Castle, Dorset, in 979, Edith is said to have turned down an offer to become Queen of England.

At the dedication of her oratory in honour of Saint Denys the Martyr (Benno decorated the murals) Saint Dunstan was supposed to have prophesied her approaching death and the incorruption of her thumb. She remained a virgin all her life and was conspicuous for her personal service to the poor and her familiarity with wild animals. She died in 984 just twenty three years of age. After her death miracles at her tomb established her cult. Not withstanding her illegitimate birth, her feast spread to many monasteries and into the Sarum Calendar. Her relics were translated in 987; from then on she, together with Saint Iwi, became Wilton's principal saints. Her feast day is 16th September.

King Canute being punished by St Edith.
By courtesy of the Royal College of Physicians.

According to William of Malmesbury, chronicler, Edith was an outspoken young lady. When St Adelward reproved her for wearing an unseemly and fine dress, she replied "I think the mind can be as pure beneath these garments adorned with gold as those beneath your dirty skins". Another story quoted by the chronicler is that when the Danish King Canute made disparaging remarks about King Edgar, an Anglo-Saxon, such as *"I would never believe a daughter of King Edgar could be a saint … he was a tyrant, a vicious man and a slave to his passions"*. Canute insisted that her tomb be opened so that he might discover what evidence of sanctity would be provided by Edith. When the tomb was opened Edith's reclining corpse was seen, with great amazement, to arise and slap Canute's face. He fell back stunned; but soon revived and was overcome with shame and created in that place a magnificent shrine in her honour. *Please see King Canute's embarrassment opposite.*

Saint Iwi (7th Century)

It is relevant to note that Saint Iwi was a Northumberland monk and a disciple of Saint Cuthbert of Lindisfarne. As a young man he decided to follow the Irish ideal of 'Exile for Christ' and took ship into the unknown. He went ashore in Brittany where he lived a life of blameless austerity as a hermit, dying on 6th October. Two or three hundred years later, a group of itinerant Breton clerics arrived at Wilton Abbey carrying Saint Iwi's relics. They were met in solemn procession by the Abbess Wulftrudis. They placed the relics on Saint Edith's altar prior to going in to supper. After enjoying the hospitality of the Abbess they discovered the reliquary had become immovable. Their tears and cries, rending of clothes and blows on the altar were alike unavailing: they were quite unable to remove the relics. Thereupon, the Abbess gave them 2,000 solidi (silver shillings) to console them for their loss and they departed. Saint Iwi's feast day is on the 8th October, presumably celebrating his translation rather than his death. It was celebrated also in Winchester, Worcester and elsewhere in S W England.

The Monk Goscelin (c. 1040-1110)

Daphne Stroud, historian, notes in the *Hatcher Review of Spring 1994*, that Goscelin was a monk, historian and a member of Bishop Hereman's household (Bishop of Sherborne and Ramsbury who moved his See to Sarum in 1075). He was born c. 1040 in Flanders and became a monk at St Bertin where Bishop Hereman, a Lorrainer, was spending a three year exile. Following his return to England Hereman sent for Goscelin to join his household at Sherborne and, from 1075, in Sarum. Bishop Hereman died in 1078 and was succeeded by Bishop Osmund (the 'Blessed', canonised in 1457) who promptly dismissed Goscelin for alleged misconduct with Eve, a young nun (born c. 1060) in the royal convent at Wilton.

Eve's father was a Danish landowner who farmed near Wilton. She was sent to the nearby royal convent to be educated with other girls from royal and aristocratic families. St Edith, above, was a former pupil. Queen Edith 'swan neck', wife of King Edward the Confessor and sister to King Harold, was also there in the 1040s. Goscelin took a personal and proper interest in the religious education of these high-born girls for whom he became a father figure. There is no evidence of any immoral conduct with Eve, a bright intelligent pupil. However there was abundant evidence of his intense 'platonic' love for her and the strict Bishop Osmund, not wishing to tolerate a scandal on his own doorstep at the very start of his episcopate, summarily dismissed him from his staff. Two years later Eve, aged about twenty, decided to escape from Goscelin's continued attentions by exchanging her comfortable home in the convent for a life of extreme austerity as an anchoress in the church of St. Lawrence at Angers in France. She died c. 1110, a much loved servant of God, whose obsequies were attended by clerks, monks, nuns, and canons.

Meanwhile Goscelin, distraught at Eve's flight to France, wandered from monastery to monastery writing about the lives of saints (including St Edith) eventually settling in Canterbury where he was still living in 1107. He was highly regarded by his contemporaries as a scholar and musician – William of Malmesbury (c. 1095 – 1147) described him as "second to none since Bede".

Wilton Abbey Fades Away: Long live Wilton House

Wilton Abbey's fortunes flourished and waned over the next 300 years or so. Royal support ensured a steady income and added the ownership of many other estates around southern England. It joined the abbeys of Shaftesbury and Winchester in importance. But royal patronage came at the expense of increasingly large royal demands for financial contributions towards the cost of the Crusades, the monarchs' disasters in France and continuous unrest at home. Eventually, Commissioners had to be called in and, on 28th March 1539, Shaftesbury Abbey and Wilton Abbey were surrendered to them. Wilton Abbey's once splendid buildings were in a ruinous state and were granted by King Henry VIII to Sir William Herbert, Earl of Pembroke, who had married Anne Parr, sister of Queen Katherine, sixth wife of the King. The Earl pulled down the abbey buildings and replaced them with today's Wilton House.

Chapter Two

The Anarchy (c. 1135-1154). The Anjou/Plantagenet Dynasty. Myths and Legends Concerning William Longespée's Birth c. 1167. His Early Life, His Family and His D'Evreux Family Relations. Bradenstoke Priory. William Marries the Young Countess Ela de Vitre, and Receives the (Third) Earldom of Salisbury. His Loyalty to King John. A Great English Naval Victory 1213. The Pope's Interdict 1208-13/14. The Defeat of the Allies at the Battle of Bouvines 1214, Earl William is Captured and Tardily Ransomed by King John. Philip II, the King of France.

The Anarchy (1135-54)

On the death of King Henry I (House of Normandy) in 1135, King Stephen of the House of Blois, seized the throne of England to the exclusion of 'Empress' Matilda (1102-67), only daughter of the late King Henry I and his wife (another) Matilda (1080-1118), daughter of King Malcolm III of Scotland. Whereupon England was plunged into a prolonged civil war (more appropriately regarded by historians as the Anarchy) during which Matilda fought to rescue England from the clutches of her usurping cousin Stephen. In 1138 the Scots, under King David I, invaded England in support of 'the Empress Matilda'; but were defeated at the Battle of Northallerton (some 10,000 Scots were killed – there were no more Scottish invasions of England for nearly two hundred years, according to *Carter's Outlines of English History*).

In 1141, Empress Matilda, widow of Henry V Holy Roman Emperor (1081-1125) and, later, wife of Geoffrey IV the Handsome 9th Count of Anjou (1015-51), who had already been proclaimed 'Queen of the Romans', was proclaimed Queen of England and 'reigned' for seven months. But she was never crowned and continued to use the title Empress by which she had become generally known in England. Her army captured King Stephen at the Battle of Lincoln; but he was soon released. Eventually, the fortunes of war did not favour her and she retired to France leaving her army to continue the war in England. In 1153 Prince Henry, Empress Matilda's son, left France to invade England and, shortly after, the Treaty of Wallingford ended 'the Anarchy' with both sides agreeing that Prince Henry would be King Stephen's successor. Stephen died the

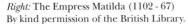

Left: Count Geoffrey or (Le Bel) of Anjou second husband of the Empress Matilda. A founder of the Anjou Dynasty and father of King Henry II. Buried at Le Mans in France.

Right: The Empress Matilda (1102 - 67) By kind permission of the British Library.

following year and Prince Henry of the House of Anjou was crowned King Henry II of England. It is interesting to note that Stephen married yet another Matilda (of Boulogne) who strongly backed his seizure of power and then became a powerful influence behind the throne during the Anarchy. She died in 1152.

The House of Anjou and Plantagenet

The earliest members of the Anjou dynasty in England were King Henry II and Empress Matilda who became a member of the House of Anjou by her second marriage. The Reverend Ben Elliott notes that when the young Geoffrey IV (1113-51) married the Empress Matilda on 2 June 1129, King Henry I hung around his neck a shield bearing little golden lions (*as in John of Marmoutier's quotation from Scott Giles Shakespeare's Heraldry p.2*). King Henry II of England was their son (and so he, too, became a member of the House of Anjou by descent).

On, or nearby, Geoffrey's tomb in the Church of St Julien at Le Mans there used to be a splendid funerary plaque of Limoges enamel depicting Count Geoffrey of Anjou c. 1150. It is now probably in the museum nearby where it shows a shield identical with that worn by William Longespée, 3rd Earl of Salisbury, as depicted also on top of the Earl's tomb in Salisbury Cathedral. David C Douglas notes that the painting involves what is probably the earliest representation of a coat of arms on shield and helmet.

King Henry II (reigned 1154-89) married Eleanor of Guienne/Aquitaine (c. 1122-1204) daughter of Duke William of Aquitaine and divorced wife of King Louis VII of France – a most intrepid lady *see page 58*. He had eleven children, three of whom were illegitimate including William Longespée, 3rd Earl of Salisbury. Among their other sons were William (1153-56); Henry (titular King of England 1170-83); King Richard Ist (r. 1189-99); Geoffrey (1158-86); and King John of England (r. 1199-1216).

The term 'House of Anjou' fell into disuse when the English lost the province of Anjou to the French. By 1154 the dynasty started to be known as Plantagenet, said to have come from the Latin planta genista, or sprig of broom, worn on Le Bel Geoffrey's hat. An alternative derivation might have come from Le Bel wearing the fur of a genet (a small catlike animal) and also worn with it a sprig of broom. The Plantagenet Dynasty itself came to an end in 1399 when that dynasty divided into the Houses of Lancaster (Red Rose faction) and York (White Rose) which combined in 1485 to become the House of Tudor till 1603 ('the Tudor Rose').

William Longespée's family origins have already been discussed in the second chapter. So, we now proceed to the circumstances of his illegitimate birth probably in the year 1167.

William Longespée was King Henry II's illegitimate son. Romantic legends state that his mother was the king's beloved mistress Rosamund (Rose of the World) de Clifford. There are indeed many myths and legends (and the names of public houses) associated with the Fair Rosamund and it seems she was the daughter of Walter de Clifford, a nobleman living in Herefordshire near the Welsh border. Henry II is said to have met her in 1165 whilst campaigning on the Welsh Marches and was entranced by her beauty. The king's consort, Eleanor of Acquitaine, who was deeply involved in plots with her sons against her husband, soon discovered the king's dalliance and, according to a legend, Henry was compelled to construct and conceal a secret love-nest for Rosamund near Woodstock in Oxfordshire. Eventually the game was up and Rosamund retired to a nunnery at Godstow, where she died early, and was buried in a magnificent grave from which she was removed in 1191 by St Hugh, the Bishop of Lincoln, because she had been the late king's mistress. She was re-interred in the abbey grounds. Her simple grave was destroyed in the 16th century.

However, Rosamund was not William's mother. Current scholarly opinion, based on careful research, is summed up by Doctor Julia Boorman, Historian and Senior Lecturer at Reading University, as follows 'two separate personal charters of William Longespée, which are in the cartulary (a collection of charters or records) of Bradenstoke Priory refer to the Countess Ida, as 'my mother' (pp 8,9 also London nos 481,646)'. Julia also notes that the *Oxford Dictionary of National Biography – ODNB –* states 'Ida was the Countess Ida de Tosni, the daughter of Roger III de Tosni, a powerful Anglo-Norman nobleman, whose wife was also called Ida. Nothing further is known of the younger Ida's relationship with King Henry but around Christmas 1181 she married Roger Bigod, 2nd Earl of Norfolk (c. 1150-1221)'.

William's parentage on both sides seems to have been widely known, indeed he proclaimed it himself. Moreover, the list of prisoners taken by the French at the Battle of Bouvines in 1214 included 'Earl William and Ralph Bigod, brother (half-brother) of the Earl of Salisbury (Moliner, 392) the younger son of Earl Roger Bigod. Ralph evidently had, and was known to have, the same mother as Earl William under whose command he was fighting'.

William was also half-brother to King Richard I The Lionheart; and to King John. He adopted the coat of arms of his paternal grandfather, Count Geoffrey, which were azure, six lioncels, or (gold); emphasising his descent from the Counts of Anjou. Julia Boorman's notes suggest that his contemporary epithet Longespée, or Lungespee, may have been a conscious invocation of his namesake William Longsword, the 2nd Duke of Normandy, during whose time his mother's family was believed to have begun its rise to prominence; and, Julia notes also, King William II was called Longespée, as well as Rufus.

His D'Evreux Family Background

The other family lineage essential to our story is that of D'Evreux (said to have evolved from the French 'l heureux' meaning 'the fortunate'). Part of the family originally came to England from France before, during, and after the Conquest of 1066. Early recorded history of the 11th century indicates that some of the D'Evreux family settled in Wiltshire and that Edward, whose name appears as Edward de Sarisberie, a major landholder in Wiltshire, in the *Domesday Book of 1086* had, by 1080, become the Sheriff of Wiltshire, an active soldier and a prosperous landowner, holding over thirty manors in the county. He was serving with Henry I in 1120.

His son, Walter D'Evreux, also became Sheriff of Wiltshire and a patron and benefactor of Sarum Cathedral. He served with King Stephen during the early part of the Anarchy (almost civil war) 1139-54. He founded the Priory at Bradenstoke, where he became a canon and on his death was buried in 1147 beside his wife, Sybil de Charworth, also called Sourches. The Priory was visited regularly by royalty and was a favourite haunt of Earl William Longespée whose daughter, Petronella, had died young and was buried there.

Walter's elder son William, another Sheriff of Wiltshire, fought for Empress Matilda during the Anarchy between King Stephen and the Empress. While he was serving in the Empress's army, and acting as Sheriff, he took part in the Earl of Gloucester's vicious attack on Wilton Abbey on 1 July 1143. He died soon after. His brother Patrick succeeded him as Constable of Sarum Castle.

Patrick, 1st Earl of Salisbury (d. 1168) was the 2nd son of Walter of Salisbury and Sybil de Charworth. His inheritance included the Domesday Honour of Chitterne in Wiltshire; in 1166 he reported more than forty knights enfeoffed on his patrimony, as well as sixteen on his mother's lands. Little is known of Maude, Patrick's first wife. He later married Adela

(Ela), daughter of Guillaume Talvas, Count of Ponthieu, and widow of William III de Warenne, 3rd Earl of Surrey (d. 1148), they had a son named William.

During the early years of the Anarchy, Patrick was loyal to King Stephen; but his nearby kinsman, John Marshal, was actively supporting the Empress in his capacity as castellan of Marlborough Castle. Eventually, the two rivals settled their differences and John Marshal married Patrick's sister Sibyl. Whereupon, Patrick changed sides and fought for Matilda. By 1147, Empress Matilda had made Patrick the lst Earl of Salisbury, after which he seized the Bishop of Winchester's castle and extensive land at Downton, a feat for which he and his men were ex-communicated. Patrick also seems to have served the Empress as Sheriff, and even to have accounted to an Angevin exchequer for the royal revenues of Wiltshire; Julia Boorman notes that he is the only baron for whom there is evidence of such a practice, and that he may have coined his own money during the Anarchy, as did a number of his contemporaries.

In 1153 Earl Patrick was present at Wallingford for the signing for the Treaty of Peace and Succession by which Matilda's son, Henry of Anjou, was named as Stephen's successor. King Stephen died in the following year. Henry was crowned King Henry II and Patrick retained his earldom and joined the new king's household continuing his service as Sheriff until 1160.

In 1168 Patrick was given responsibility for Poitou province in France jointly with Queen Eleanor. 'One day', according to historian *David Crouch's 'William Marshal' London 1990 p.35*, 'while escorting Queen Eleanor on a peaceful expedition between castles in France, the party was ambushed by Guy and Geoffrey de Lusignan and an armed group. Their aim was to capture the Queen and hold her to ransom. Patrick put her on a fast horse, slapped its rump, and told her to ride to the safety of a ruined castle nearby. During the ensuing fight, Patrick was stabbed in the back before he could put on his hauberk (protective body armour) and he died of his wounds. The recently knighted 22 year old William (later to become William The Marshal, Earl of Pembroke) was a nephew of Earl Patrick and had joined the party. He was left to hold off the Lusignans. Unfortunately, he was cornered by them against a hedge and was wounded by a slash from behind and captured. The Queen ransomed William, whose wounds the Lusignans had refused to dress, and took him into her retinue. William became a close friend of the Queen and she arranged for him to take over as Master of the Household of Prince Henry, the Queen's second son (also styled as the titular King of England, or the Young King (1170-83) who died early).

For more details of William The Marshal and his family, please see Chapter Five.

William, son of Earl Patrick (also called William FitzPatrick i.e. Fitz from the Latin filius, son, then French fils), succeeded to the earldom in 1168. Much later on he too became Sheriff of Wiltshire and was loyal to King Henry II and then King Richard I, whose coronation was quickly planned to prevent his brother John from seizing the throne for himself, where he bore the sceptre and the dove. Shortly after at Richard's crown-wearing ceremony at Winchester in 1194 he carried a sword of state and was one of four earls carrying the canopy. He fought during campaigns in Wales and Normandy. In about 1190, he married Ela née De Vitre, daughter of Richard de Vitre and widow of Gilbert Crespin, Lord Tillieres (who died in c. 1190 during the 3rd Crusade in the Holy Land). Within a year their daughter Ela was born, probably in one of the baronial manors on the banks of the River Avon. Earl William died in 1196 when Ela was about five years old, leaving her heiress to her father's title of earl, i.e. she became a Countess suo jure (in her own right) and received the custodianship of the royal castle at Sarum and much more besides.

For Abridged Family Trees of the Longespée and D'Evreux Families, please see pages 143-145.

Bradenstoke Priory. Medieval Home of the Longespée, D'Evreux and Marshal families

Bradenstoke – cum Clack village is located in northwest Wiltshire on a high ridge of land overlooking the beautiful Avon valley. RAF Lyneham airfield and the small country town of Royal Wootton Bassett are nearby – the latter was the scene of spontaneous expressions of family and public grief as the bodies of soldiers killed during the war in Afghanistan were driven away for burial near their family homes.

Bradenstoke's Augustinian Priory of Clack, dedicated to St Mary, was founded in 1139 by Walter D'Evreux. It was visited regularly by Angevin royalty and was a favourite haunt of Earl William Longespée.

Bradenstoke Priory c. late 19 century.

Ruins of Bradenstoke Priory 2010.

The original priory was a daughter house of St Mary's Abbey in Cirencester. Its local charter was confirmed in 1139 by Walter's wife, Sybil, and his sons Patrick and William, in the presence of Bishop Roger of Sarum. As the priory grew in wealth and importance, it broke away from its mother abbey and flourished in its own right; eventually extending its property and interest into eight counties in south and middle England. Earl Patrick's body, following his murder by the Lusignan brothers, was brought back from Normandy in 1168 and was also buried at the priory which continued to be patronised by the D'Evreux family, the Marshal (Pembroke) family, the Longespée family and by royalty. King Henry II's own (royal) charter c. 1175 confirmed the spiritual and temporal endowments of the priory. King John visited the priory on nine occasions between the years 1200 and 1214. Later on, the Holy Abbess of Lacock Abbey, Countess Ela, maintained a continuing interest in the affairs of the priory and gave it a stream of substantial gifts.

It is interesting to note that many of the great names associated with Bradenstoke Priory, at this time, supported the Empress Matilda in the civil war (the Anarchy) against King Stephen. It is curious, also, how most of the two warring factions came together after the death of Stephen and loyally served his son King Henry II.

It is even more curious to note the variety of Anglo-Saxon words which were used to explain the requirements of the feudal system. For example, in 1232, three royal charters confirm the ownership of the priory and listed various grants given to the owners such as 'soc and sac, toil and team, infangthef and utfangthef, quittance from all geld, and from suit in shire, hundred, and wafentake courts ..... and from ward penny, over penny and tithing penny, and from henigwyte, flemenwyte, leirwyte, blocwyte, grethbreche, forstall, hamsoc, heiborum and frankpledge – Ministry of Agriculture civil servants, please note.

The main building survived into recent times (see photographs on page 27); but in 1928/29 the priory was mostly demolished. Its great tithe barn and impressive guest house were acquired by the American newspaper millionaire, William Randolph Hearst. They were dismantled stone by stone, crated up and carted away. The barn was shipped to America for re-erection on Hearst's modern castle estate in San Simeon, California; but he soon lost interest in his project and sold the stones to a local hotelier, who intended to re-build the tithe barn on his property as a venue for holding wedding receptions. However, planning permission was refused because of local earthquake restrictions on height. Since then, the stones have been rediscovered in America still in their original shipping crates, unloved and forlorn.

The guest house stones were taken to Randolph Hearst's recent acquisition, St Donat's castle near Cowbridge, Glamorgan. Here, squeezed between the inner and outer castle curtains, there is a fine building called Bradenstoke Hall. Its name and 12th century stones – mainly at roof level – proclaim their origin in Wiltshire. St Donat's castle is now the home of Atlantic College founded by Kurt Hahn, the international educationalist.

There are a couple of delightful medieval houses in Bradenstoke village nearby, one of which is said by villagers to have had associations with the priory (possibly, they say, to house the retinues of important visitors).

The sad remains of this large and splendid religious house are maintained with the help of a small grant from English Heritage to ensure safety of visitors on site. All the larger buildings have gone, leaving the remains of what appears to have been an Italianate tower, probably of a slightly later date, encrusted with bushes from the apex of which a flag flutters defiantly in the wind – more to welcome occasional visitors, perhaps, than in hope of rescue and recovery of the property. Views around are superb, the grass is neatly cut, the hedges nicely shaped, horses trot about in nearby paddocks and a proud little avenue of trees denotes where even the foundations of the priory's nave, (only twenty four feet wide, by a hundred and twenty six feet long), have been removed. Further investigations reveal a dark mysterious undercroft in which to test the visitors' imagination and courage.

An archaeological dig, sometime ago, revealed a curious cemetery of eight tombs laid out in the form of a star – eight heads in a central circle with eight bodies and sixteen legs laid out towards the circumference.

The original placement of the Prior's intricately carved fireplace may be suspected somewhere above the undercroft; but accurate confirmation is impossible for the original was rescued and moved to safety by a member of the Methuen family and taken to their home in nearby Corsham Court. It is now in a somewhat disintegrated state.

William Longespée is Betrothed to Ela D'Evreux and Created Third Earl of Salisbury. He Marries Ela Ten Years Later.

King Richard I sought to take the young Ela as his ward. Her mother, fearing her husband's brothers, took her to the safety of her family's lands in France. According to the Lacock Abbey register (Monastrum vol VI, p.501), William Talbot, a knight of the King's court, dressed as a pilgrim, discovered Ela and her mother in a French castle. He transformed himself from pilgrim to troubadour, entered the castle and succeeded in persuading the two runaways to return to England. Julia Boorman, current history source, says that the truth of this story is unclear.

It is doubtful whether Ela remained with her mother for, in 1198, the latter entered into her fourth marriage, to Gilbert de Mailsmaine, probably having arranged for Ela to be looked after by a noblewoman in the king's court. According to the *Oxford Dictionary of National Biography*, and *the Complete Peerage*, King Richard I, while campaigning in Normandy 1196-97, arranged for his ward, the Countess Ela, then about six years old, to be betrothed to William Longespée. Julia Boorman notes that William Earl of Salisbury is entered at the head of the account for Michaelmas 1196 Wiltshire in the *Pipe Roll of the 8th year of Richard I's reign*; but an allowance to him for custody of the castle at Sarum was only for half a year (*Pipe Roll 8. Richard I. Pipe Roll Soc p.23-24*) – this would be at the time Ela's father, the previous Earl of Salisbury, died. The following year, Michaelmas 1197, 'William, brother of the king, received the third penny of Wiltshire by writ of the king' according to *Pipe Roll 9. Richard I. PRS p.207-8* (receiving the third penny was the perquisite of the earl of a county). Thus William became the Third Earl of Salisbury. Their formal marriage probably took place when Ela reached her sixteenth birthday in c1207; but the exact date is unknown and may have been earlier.

The marriage was soon consummated and, during the next fourteen years, she bore him eight surviving children. It seems that she lived her life in Sarum or the surrounding countryside where she would have had more relations and friends with whom she could stay in the absence of her husband on his frequent travels abroad. In the *Register of St Osmund*, the Countess Ela is described as *'a woman indeed worthy of praise because she was filled with the fear of the Lord'*.

His Loyalty to King John and his Early Military Service

William was in close attendance on King Richard from 1196-98. He received the town of Appleby in Lincolnshire from the king in 1198. He attended his half-brother John's coronation on 27 May 1199 and became his close confidant. Ancient manuscripts in *Salisbury Cathedral's archives* describe William Longespée as *'a man of infinite courage and one of the best soldiers that England had bred, in so much as King John did command that his son Henry (born 1 October 1207 and later to become King Henry III 1216-72) should be trained up by him in the military arts'*. He played an important part in diplomatic and political missions at home and abroad on behalf of his monarch. He was appointed Lieutenant of Gascony; Sheriff of Wiltshire (which he held on three separate occasions); Constable of Dover Castle; Warden of the Cinque Ports; Warden of the Welsh Marches; a number of sheriffdoms including those of Cambridge, Huntingdon, Lincoln, Somerset, Hampshire, Staffordshire and Shropshire; the governorship of several important royal castles such as Winchester, Eye, Dover, Porchester, Sherborne and Southampton; he was Marshal of the English armies and Commander of the English fleet – all for varying periods of time. He was also appointed supervisor of the keeper of the archbishopric of Canterbury in 1212 and received the baronry of Trowbridge in 1213 after the King confiscated Henry de Bohun's land and possessions.

Contemporary sources (*Rot de Lb Pipe Roll and 5 John. pp.139-40. Painter's King John p.40 and W L Warren's King John pp.108,180*) tell us that *'King John gave William an annual pension, against which William frequently borrowed more money from the King'*. Also (*'King John liked to send William a tun or two of wine'*), (a tun was the Gaulish name for a large cask or barrel), *'play cards with him, and lend him a few silver marks when gambling left him out of pocket'* (a mark was a measure of gold or silver; a silver mark was worth the equivalent of thirteen shillings and four pence; and a gold mark about six pounds). 'King John' (a widely-read monarch whose family would have been well aware of the common people's opinion that *an unlettered king is a crowned ass) 'had a small library which he carried around with him in his baggage train. Once, John borrowed books from the Abbot of Reading and lent him, in return, a copy of Pliny the Elder, the Roman naturalist AD 28-79'*, who died in an eruption of Vesuvius. In the spring of 1205, when John was at Windsor, *he asked Reginald of Cornhill to send him two tuns of wine and a History of England written in French. The king paid to John of Kempsey for chests and carts to carry his books (Libris Regis) overseas. When not reading, he often liked to spend a leisure moment playing games of chance with William Longespée'.*

William accompanied the King to Normandy in 1201 and, on several occasions, commanded the English armies in France. In 1204, accompanied by William The Marshal, he escorted Llewellyn Prince of Wales to meet the King at Worcester. The King also sent him on a diplomatic mission to Germany which ended successfully when King John's nephew, Otto of Saxony and Brunswick (also Emperor of Germany and Holy Roman Emperor), supported King John's aspirations in his region. In 1205 he saw active service with the garrison of La Rochelle in NW France. In 1208 he was appointed Keeper of the March of Wales and in 1210 he accompanied King John on a large expedition to Ireland. Whilst he was in command of the fleet in 1213 English spies reported that a large French fleet, assembled by England's enemy King Philip II (Philip Augustus, King of France from 1180-1223) for the invasion of England, was lying unguarded off the coast of Flanders; and also that Philip and his army were away besieging the inland town of Ghent. King John sent Longespée in command of five hundred ships to take the French by surprise.

A Great English Naval Victory off the Port of Damme

On 13 May 1213 William Longespée swept across the English Channel and discovered the unsuspecting French fleet off the port of Damme, NE of Bruges. He attacked at once capturing three hundred French ships heavily laden with arms, provisions and the belongings of French nobles. He sent them over to England with prize crews and then burned one hundred ships drawn up along the shore. *'Never since the days of King Arthur'*, said *the nearly contemporary biographer of William The Marshall in his 'Histoire', 'did so much booty come into England'.* Next day he attacked the ships in the harbour and the town of Damme itself. Thereupon King Philip rushed back with a strong force causing Longespée, on 1 June, to evacuate the town, reach his ships in safety and then return home in triumph. A great English naval victory which certainly put paid to any plans Philip may have had for invading England at that time. Moreover, King Philip, unable to get the remaining transports out of the area was obliged to burn them lest they fell prey to another English sortie.

The Pope's Interdict over England and Wales 1208-13. Longespée's Reaction.

Pope Innocent III laid an interdict over England and Wales during the period 1208-13/14 following King John's refusal to allow the Pope's nominee (Stephen Langton, then the English Chancellor of the University of Paris) to occupy the vacant Metropolitan See at Canterbury. This interdict permitted no ecclesiastical office save that of baptism of infants and last rites for the dying, however, some priories found it possible to celebrate quietly and without the ringing of bells. It had no formal legal backing, was extremely general and tended to punish the innocent as well the guilty. Bishops consulted one another; Herbert

Poore, Bishop of Salisbury, asked the chapter of St Paul's what they thought. (*W L Warren. King John p.170*). It seems likely that the Pope, somewhat naively, expected John to submit quickly. But John did not; and he was supported by the laity and many of the clergy and monks. *Warren also says King John (p.268) retaliated by confiscating church property and even ordered all the clergy's housekeepers, hearthmates, bossy mistresses, lady-loves (amasiae) with their creaking cradles and squalling brats to be seized and held for ransom. Many of them hurried to bail out their womenfolk.* Gerald of Wales the chronicler confirms.

Longespée's reaction was to support the king and he advised him 'To reject the interdict and pay no attention to the Pope's Menaces'. Suiting action to words William played a ferocious part against the king's enemies. Meanwhile the Pope excommunicated King John in 1209 and, losing his patience, declared in 1212 that John should be deposed and he seems to have authorised King Philip of France to carry out the deposition (however, the historian C.R. Cheney regards this deposition as 'unproven').

Eventually, in 1213, John negotiated a deal with the ageing, but still active, Pope (who died three years later) and agreed to become his vassal. He allowed Langton to return and become Archbishop. He agreed also to restore all confiscated church property and to pay an annual tribute of 1,000 marks to the Pope. He undertook to support the Pope's plans for a new Crusade in the Middle East and, it seems, took the Cross (which must have terrified the English barons, who feared a massive increase in taxes needed to fund a subsequent Crusade). However, there is no evidence of John's presence on any Crusade. William was one of the earls who swore that John would observe the Papal terms concerning satisfaction to the bishops and witnessed the delegation of power to the Papal See. The Pope then lifted the interdict and ordered Philip II of France not to make war on his 'faithful vassal' – whereupon Philip, furious at the Pope's duplicity, attacked his neighbour the Count of Flanders, John's ally.

Earl William Longspée is captured by the Bishop of Beauvais during the Battle of Bouvines (Comic History of England, John Leech artist c. 1860).

The Battle of Bouvines 27 July 1214. Earl William is Captured and Ransomed.

During the period from late 1213 to the middle of 1214 King John, in alliance with the imperial allies led by Otto IV the Holy Roman Emperor, Renaud de Dammartin Count of Boulogne and Ferrand Count of Flanders, was in France at war with King Philip II of France. John's strategy was to draw Philip's army southwards away from Paris so that Emperor Otto, commanding the main army from the low countries, could march on Paris. But Otto's army was slow to move and Philip forced John to retire further south into Aquitaine where he remained far away from the impending battle.

King Philip then counter-marched north and chose to fight Otto and the imperial allies on the plain at Bouvines near the river Marque. The French had an army of 15,000 men of whom 11,000 were infantry and 4,000 were cavalry. The Allies had about 25,000 foot soldiers, but rather less cavalry than the French. Emperor Otto commanded the centre of the Allies' Army. William Longespée and Renaud de Dammartin Count of Boulogne commanded the Allies' right flank and Ferrand Count of Flanders the left flank. Both sides adopted similar positions. Cavalry on the wings and infantry in the centre. The battle opened with a confused cavalry fight on the French right. Then the two centres clashed. As the French weakened, King Philip with his reserves went into battle and retrieved the situation, although his horse was killed under him. Meanwhile, the French left wing was victorious. William Longespée was knocked off his horse by a mace wielded by that splendid example of the church militant, Philippe of Dreux the Bishop of Beauvais, and taken prisoner together with the Count of Flanders. The final battle in the centre, led on one side by Otto, and by Philip on the other, was decided when the imperial allies turned tail and retreated – Emperor Otto's life was saved by the devotion of a few Saxon knights; but his Imperial Eagle Standard was captured by the French.

The Histoire de Guillaume le Marechal (which is a family history of William The Marshal, Earl of Pembroke, composed in verse by a Frenchman - various translations into English have followed) explicitly absolves William from any blame for the disaster at Bouvines, stating that the battle was fought against his advice, and that the Emperor Otto would have been captured or slain without Salisbury's aid.

When news of King Philip's victory reached Paris, French students are said to have danced with joy up and down the streets of Paris for a whole week; whilst restless rebel English barons at home noted with relief King John's military weakness and lost no time in preparing their demands on King John i.e. the Articles of the Barons.

King Henry II of England attending the Coronation of Phillip II Auguste of France 1180.

Ferrand, Count of Flanders, remained in a French prison until 1227. Renaud, Count of Boulogne languished in a French prison until about 1229 when he committed suicide.

William Longespée was held by the French and remained in captivity until February 1215 when negotiations began for his release in exchange for Robert, son of the Count of Dreux. By May of that year William was back in England and had been appointed to examine the state of the royal castles; but his attempt to prevent London falling into the hands of the rebel barons was unsuccessful. A short while later he was despatched to Devon, with a force of Flemish mercenaries, against a group of English rebels and successfully forced the rebels to abandon Exeter. His presence at Runnymede on 15 June 1215 is doubtful. But he was one of the 'venerable fathers' whose advice would be sought by King John in the introductory paragraph of Magna Carta before he affixed his seal. He probably joined King John on around 19 June. He received extensive grants from the royal demesne in August in compensation for the honour of Trowbridge, restored to Henry de Bohun by the provisional committee of twenty five because of the king's previous unjust decision.

King Philip II (Philip Augustus 1165-1223). Son of Louis VII r. 1180-1223.

From the moment he succeeded to the throne of France he set about uniting the warring factions in Northern France; and then turned his attention to driving the English out of France. He allied himself with Prince Richard (later King Richard the Lionheart), the rebellious eldest son of King Henry II, and continued the enlargement of his kingdom. Following the death of King Henry II, Philip and Richard the Lionheart embarked on the 3rd Crusade. But soon after the capture of Cyprus and the important mainland port of Acre, they quarrelled. Philip decided to return to France and Richard decided to return to England: on his way back he was captured by King Leopold of Austria and was released seventeen months later having paid a sum said to have been three times his annual income. After Richard's death in 1199, King Philip launched a well planned and executed war on King John's possessions in France. He captured Normandy (but not the Channel Islands), Brittany, Anjou, Maine, Turaine and then Poitou. Thus breaking up the great Anjou Norman Empire for good, and ensured the subsequent unity of France.

Saint Philip Auguste
King of France.

King Philip II Auguste King
of France 1165 - 1223.
r. 1180 - 1223.

Chapter Three

Background. Start of the Revolt. The Articles of the Barons. King John Seals Magna Carta. Main Clauses. Deletions and Amendments. Civil War Starts. Pope Innocent III Intervenes. Prince Louis of France Invades England. King John Dies 1216.

Background

King John's series of defeats on the continent during 1214 at the hands of King Louis Philip of France, and his consequent lack of military strength, encouraged the rebel barons of England in their disagreement with John. Moreover, John's revived political relations with the Pope in Rome, together with expected tax rises to finance the Pope's intention to launch a fresh Crusade in the Middle East and John's decision to 'take the Cross' on 14 March 1215 would certainly have concentrated the minds of the barons and underlined their need to act as soon as possible.

Start of the Revolt and The Articles of the Barons

King John in his prime
(Players' cigarettes).

Militant northern barons met secretly at St Albans and St Paul's Cathedral in 1213 and at Bury St Edmunds in 1214. With the support of Stephen Langton, Archbishop of Canterbury, they resolved to remind King John of his coronation oaths; and to demand his agreement to an undated list of forty nine points entitled *'The Articles of the Barons'*; King John's seal of approval was affixed to this document at Runnymede; although the document itself is undated. It is interesting to note that these Articles were once held by Gilbert Burnet, Bishop of Salisbury 1689-1715, and are now on display in the British Library. Meanwhile the rebel barons had already seized the Tower and City of London and the Exchequer on 17th March 1215 and had renounced their allegiance to the King. But they failed to capture Windsor castle.

King John in a Bate, from the
Comic History of England by G A A
Beckett, illustrated by John Leech,
published by Routledge c. 1850.

The Meeting between King John and the Barons at Runnymede

After much procrastination the king met the rebel barons in a meadow on the south bank of the river Thames called Runnymede, between Windsor and Staines. Detailed negotiations based on the 49 Articles of the Barons, probably staged and influenced by William The Marshal Earl of Pembroke and Archbishop Langton, resulted in King John, after joining the rebel barons in a formal ceremony of acceptance, putting his seal on what became the 63 clauses of Magna Carta. It was nominally dated 15th June 1215 and was prepared by the Royal Chancery clerks.

A further ceremony took place on 19 June, says W L Warren, author of King John 1997 Estate edition p.236, at which the rebels formally renewed their oaths of allegiance to the king. Modern research indicates that thirteen exemplifications were made of Magna Carta (seven by 24th June, and six by brief patent on 22nd July) of which Elias de Dereham, senior member of the Archbishop's secretariat (Steward), was given ten of these copies for distribution (four on 24th June and all six on 22nd July). One of these exemplifications was probably sent to Earl William Longespée, the Sheriff of Wiltshire, at Sarum castle. It seems likely that at least forty exemplifications were intended for distribution throughout England. However the start of the civil war, and an early harvest, may have interrupted these plans.

King John Seals Magna Carta

The Salisbury Magna Carta is by far the best written of the three originals extant, others are in Lincoln Castle, on loan from Lincoln Cathedral, and the other is in the British Library. A fourth survivor was badly burnt in the Cotton Library Fire on 23rd October 1731: however it was still possible, then, to read the text and, by order of the Speaker of the House of Commons, an almost perfect transcription was made of this copy in 1732 and this is also on display in the British Library. Unfortunately the burnt copy has since deteriorated and is now illegible though it still retains a forlorn remnant of King John's double-sided seal. These four exemplifications are of different size, shape and handwriting with slight variations on the text. Claire Breay of the British Library states 'the Salisbury copy differs from the others in that it is not written by the hand of a Royal Chancery scribe. But it may have been presented for authorisation under the Great Seal – its text is as authentic as the other three and has equal authority with them.

It may be relevant here to note that Daphne Stroud, in her article of the June 2000 issue of Salisbury Cathedral News, raised three questions regarding the Salisbury exemplification. Firstly, she says, that the handwriting differs from the style of writing usually associated with chancery documents of the period; secondly, the unusual pattern of seal holes raises doubts about the presence of a seal and, thirdly, a 14th century clerk has written the word 'dupplicatur' (it is duplicated) on the back of a number of documents presently in Salisbury Cathedral archives, including Magna Carta, which suggests it was one of two copies then in Salisbury.

The Salisbury Charter measures 14x17¼ inches or 35cm x 43cm. It is written on vellum (animal skin) in medieval Latin with 'shorthand' abbreviations (to save space) e.g. the single letter q replaces qui, qua, quo etc. meaning who, which or what; and roots of verbs replace longer third person plurals. The changes being indicated by a line drawn over the shorter version. There are about three thousand five hundred words in seventy six lines of text. The justification is perfect with no irregular spaces between words. It is a truly beautiful work of medieval art. The Great Seal is missing but the place from which it may have hung is clearly visible. The ink used was probably a water-based mixture which included oakapple

King John's effigy flanked by 2 Bishops. V&A Cast Court.

(the gall of the oak tree which produced the dark colour), iron nitrate to bite into the vellum thus preventing subsequent alterations of the text and was bound together by fish glue, tree gum or albumen (white of eggs). The writer would have been very experienced in the writing and production of documents and he would have used a quill.

It is clear that the original wording of Magna Carta was the work of many people and put together hurriedly by the chancery clerks. King John had already accepted the Articles of the Barons shortly before the final meeting at Runnymede; but William The Marshal the Elder (Earl of Pembroke) and Archbishop Stephen Langton were still endeavouring to exert a moderating influence on the intemperate crafty king and his greedy rebellious barons. In this context it is interesting to note that Langton was able to insert an important fresh introduction, not previously mentioned in the Articles, which confirmed the liberty of the English church. Another amendment was the substitution of the words 'any baron' by the words 'any freeman' in clause 39, thus significantly enlarging Magna Carta's scope. A solitary favourable mention of the hapless underrepresented social classes below freeman occurs in clause 20 regarding the fairness of amercements (fines in a court of law).

Main Clauses of Magna Carta

These are:

> The right of the Church to govern its own affairs free from Royal interference.
>
> Limits imposed on unfair demands under the feudal system.
>
> No man to be fined (amerced) without a fair trial by his equals.
>
> Punishments to be in proportion to the gravity of the offence; but not so heavy as to deprive a man of his livelihood (he should be allowed to keep the tools of his trade).
>
> Freedom of the City of London to enjoy ancient liberties and customs.
>
> Freedom of travel for merchants and others.
>
> Standardisation of weights and measures.
>
> Repeal of many harsh forest laws and punishments.
>
> The removal of weirs and enclosures of riverbanks (to facilitate navigation of rivers).
>
> Restoration of lands, estates, castles and liberties to those unlawfully dispossessed.
>
> Return of hostages and removal (repatriation) of foreign officials and mercenaries.
>
> Protection for widows, heirs and dependants.
>
> The King was not above the law.
>
> And finally, those magnificent words 'To none shall we deny, to none shall we delay, to none shall we refuse justice'.

Some Important Deletions from the Charter

The revolutionary provision in Clause 61 of the 1215 Magna Carta for a Standing Council of twenty five leading figures in the country to enforce the monarch's implementation of the laws, with powers to 'call out the community of the whole land' and to seize his castles, land and possessions sparing only his life and family', was omitted from all subsequent versions. In 1354, the words 'no freeman' in clause 39 were substituted by 'no man of whatsoever state or condition he may be'. This important change, together with the effects of the Black Death c. 1349 on the labour market and the Peasants Revolt of 1381, heralded the collapse of the feudal system in England and the emergence of a parliamentary democracy based on freedom from tyranny for all people.

The forest laws were taken out in 1217 and expanded. At this time, the original Charter became known as the Great Charter, or Magna Carta, and was so named because it was larger in comparison with the Forest Charter.

Subsequent Amendments and Revisions of Magna Carta

The laws contained in the 1215 version of Magna Carta were observed for barely two months and then King John, the Rebel Barons and the Pope ignored them completely. How ironic, therefore, when two years later, it was brought back as a royal manifesto warmly welcomed by the barons and fully accepted by the new Pope (Honorious III).

William The Marshal issued the first revised version of Magna Carta on 12 November 1216 and another on 6 November 1217.

Having reached his majority, King Henry III took over control of the country from Hubert de Burgh and the Regency Council. He issued the third amended Charter in 1225 using his own Great Seal. There is an excellent exemplar of the 1225 Charter in the British Library and others are in Durham Cathedral and the Public Record Office at Kew. Henry III confirmed the Charter again in 1237, in 1253 and in 1265. His son, King Edward I, agreed that many of the provisions of his father's Charter should be placed on the Statute Book in 1297. Early exemplifications are in the British Library, the City of London Guildhall, the Public Record Office at Kew, the National Library in Canberra, Australia and the National Archives Rotunda of the Library of Congress in Washington DC. In December 2007 the Washington Magna Carta was sold by the Ross Perot Foundation for 10.6 million pounds to the American lawyer and businessman David Rubenstein, who intends it to remain on display in the National Archives.

The provisions of Magna Carta were quoted and misquoted in the days leading to the regicides of 1649 in England (Charles I) and 1793 in France (Louis XVI); and have since been raised during many constitutional debates around the world.

In his essay 'Magna Carta in American Law', published in c. 2000. David Stivison points out that nine hundred decisions by federal and state courts in the USA referred to Magna Carta for guidance. In over one hundred decisions, the United States

King John's Seals as Commander-in-Chief (top) and as Head of State.

Supreme Court had explained American dependence on Magna Carta for an understanding of the due process of law – a speedy and public trial before an unbiased judge and jury of peers, and protection against excessive bail or fines or cruel or unusual punishments. During the period 1940 – 2000 over sixty United States Supreme Court cases produced comment and commentary on Magna Carta's role in US law.

It is interesting to observe that, when the Australians built their second new parliament building, they placed a grass lawn over its curving roof and encouraged the citizenary to walk up, sit down and picnic on the roof. Thus, they said, Magna Carta showed that King John was not above the law; and the new roof reminds the Australian politicians below that they are not above the people (sadly, the Australian public are no longer allowed, for security reasons, to roam around the roof of their parliament building).

William Shakespeare does not mention Magna Carta in his play 'King John', though he does mention, in another context, William Longespée, Earl of Salisbury; Hubert de Burgh, Earl of Kent; and William The Marshal, Earl of Pembroke and, for good measure, a Bastard too (Act IV, Scenes 1 & 3). *See also page 50 for the complete quotation.*

In the words of the British Library authorities 'the Great Charter of 1215 was a landmark in the transition from an oral to a written society. It has become the practical starting point of our social and political history by reason of its clarity, comprehensiveness and skilful attention to detail. It provided a legal basis for the future development of such fundamental rights as trial by jury, Habeas Corpus, equality before the law, freedom from arbitrary arrests, parliamentary control of taxation and independence of the Church free from royal interference.

Pope Innocent III Intervenes

Although an uneasy peace had been reached between the barons and their monarch to enable formal negotiations to take place it did not last long. Both sides refused to disarm, suspicion was in the air and the accord between them broke down irretrievably. The royal army failed to recapture London which remained with the rebel barons. In July 1215 King John appealed to Pope Innocent III on the grounds that he had been forced to agree and asked the Pope to amend the Charter. The Pope did so on 24th August 1215 by way of a bull declaring Magna Carta null and void. Thus Magna Carta was the law of the land for only ten weeks. The Pope also ordered Archbishop Langton to excommunicate the rebel barons; but he refused and was suspended by the Papal Legate and the Bishop of Winchester. Greatly disappointed, Langton went to France in exile. Meanwhile Elias de Dereham joined the rebel barons at Winchester preaching that the Pope's actions were unlawful because the Pope had not been informed of the true facts; therefore, he argued, the rebellion was perfectly legal, because King John had broken his solemn undertakings.

Prince Louis, Dauphin of France, Leads the Rebel Barons. King John Dies.

The rebel barons, who now controlled London and most of the south east including Winchester, decided to appoint a leader and offered the crown of England to Prince Louis, son and heir of King John's old enemy King Philip II of France. (Prince Louis later became King Louis VIII and father of the canonised Louis IX, commander of the ill-fated Seventh Crusade 1248-54, of whom more anon). Prince Louis accepted the offer. The advance party of Frenchmen landed in London November 1215 and Prince Louis joined them on 21 May 1216. Louis had his own reasons for 'invading' England. He claimed the English throne for himself through his wife Blanche, a grand-daughter of King Henry II and King John's niece, who, later, became Queen of France and her country's much respected Regent during various absences abroad of her son. This gave Louis some respectability. About two thirds of the English barons went over to Prince Louis – but they had no siege trains. Some one hundred and fifty castles supported King John and he was able to recruit swarms of mercenaries.

Meanwhile, in July 1216, news was received in Winchester of the death of the aged, but still powerful, Pope Innocent III. His successor had not yet been elected (perhaps, no smoke from the Vatican chimney). A new situation was developing fast.

No bishop could be found to crown Prince Louis King of England and the barons seemed strangely reluctant to fight an all-out civil war. King John marched around the country and on to the Scottish border and back to Lincolnshire where he lost his baggage train and much of the royal regalia and treasure in quicksands around The Wash (it is still being sought today). Then King John suddenly fell ill, the Abbot of Croxton heard his confession and performed the last rites. King John died of dysentery and over-exhaustion, aged forty nine, in the neighbourhood of Swinestead Abbey near Newark castle on 18th October 1216. His splendid tomb is in Worcester Cathedral.

Chapter Four

Young King Henry III is Crowned. The Civil War Continues. Earl William Longespée Supports King John, then Changes Sides Twice. He Takes Part in the Battle of Lincoln Fair. Another Great English Naval Victory. Prince Louis is Defeated and Returns to France. Peace is Restored.

> *"If Prince Louis captures England, I will carry the little king on my shoulders from island to island and country to country and will never leave him, even if I have to beg for bread".*
> WILLIAM THE MARSHAL (THE ELDER), EARL OF PEMBROKE, REGENT OF ENGLAND.

King Henry III is Crowned

King John's death changed the political situation dramatically. For the time being it seemed that the barons were, after all, 'royalists' at heart. All eyes turned towards nine year old Prince Henry, eldest legitimate child of King John and his second wife, Isabella of Angoulême. He was described by a contemporary as a 'pretty little knight'. He was discovered living with his mother in Devizes. They took him up to Gloucester and, because the coronation crown of England was still unavailable in the Tower of London and the Archbishop of Canterbury was still in exile, Peter des Roches, Bishop of Winchester, crowned him King Henry III of England with a circlet of gold supplied by his mother (some historians say that Gualo Biechieri, the Pope's legate, also placed his gold ring on young Henry's head). This took place in St Peter's Abbey (now Gloucester Cathedral). A nearby poet noted 'the boy seemed to be a tiny spark of minute beauty, the sole hope of the torn kingdom like the Star of Bethlehem'. On 12th November 1216, at Bristol, the aged Earl of Pembroke, the Regent, in the presence of Gualo, re-issued Magna Carta in the king's name.

William Longespée's Service in the Civil War. He Changes Sides Twice.

When civil war started William supported King John energetically all over the country and was present during the cruel ravages at Ely in early 1216; however, according to the ODNB *'it was William who protected the womenfolk from the worst excesses of Walter Buc's mercenaries and, in the presence of King John, took the surrender of many French troops after the siege of Colchester'.* Then, in June 1216, before John's unexpected death later in the year he lost faith in John's cause and removed Ela and her family from Sarum to the safety of the heavily fortified castle at Devizes. Then he decided to submit to Prince Louis at Winchester and he surrendered to him the royal castle at Sarum.

According to a rumour recorded by the Chronicler, William the Breton, William's decision to change sides in June 1216 was because, in c. 1214-1215, King John had made amorous advances to the Countess Ela during the many months William had been imprisoned in France after the battle of Bouvines. But, according to the ODNB, *'little credence should be given to this biased story'.* However, the long wait for the arrival of his ransom from King John must have rankled with him: moreover, the personal relations between the two strong-willed, hot-tempered, half-brothers were not always cordial; and, more likely, many of William's friends among the nobility had already deserted King John having themselves lost faith in his cause. More likely still the fortunes of war looked like favouring Prince Louis whose forces were sallying out of London and chasing John's soldiers westwards; thus threatening William's family and interests in Wiltshire.

Now serving with Prince Louis and the rebel barons, he agreed to go to Dover and, according to the chronicler Wendover, he tried to persuade Hubert de Burgh, a strong supporter of King John, to surrender Dover castle of which he was then the warden.

Hubert refused, reproving William for acting against his royal blood. According to Mathew Paris, Hubert said *'I beseech you by the blood of Christ to allow me to hang rather than surrender the castle to any Frenchman, for it is the gate of England giving access to Kent and London'*.

On 5 March 1217, during the absence of Prince Louis in France, William Longespée changed sides again. This time William was motivated by the unexpected death of King John and the Royal Council's decision to offer the throne of England to young Prince Henry, John's son and William's nephew. Moreover, the fresh opportunities for him in the young king's court would have seemed irresistible and the safety and welfare of his family would be assured. Furthermore, during the amicable negotiations which followed, he was promised the ownership of Sherborne castle and extensive land in Somerset and Devon. As Linda K Jack, the historian, points out in a quote from David Carpenter's history, *'An Earl without his own castle is almost as bad as a Knight without a horse'*.

He accepted an invitation to join the young King Henry III's Council at Oxford and rejoined the royal army bringing with him his kinsman, William Marshal, the Younger, and a contingent of English soldiers from Wiltshire and the South West. Their defection was a major blow to Prince Louis whose military position soon began to worsen by the day. The English armies captured Knipp castle near Shoreham and the fortified episcopal palace at Wolvesey; Southampton surrendered to the royal army and Louis handed over the city of Winchester, together with a great deal of valuable booty. The custodianship of the royal castle at Sarum was returned to Longespée by the King's Council at this time.

Above left: Queen Isabella of Angoulême. Second wife of King John, Mother of Henry III d. 1246.
Above right: King Henry III r. 1216 - 1272 Both photos taken at V&A Cast Court.

The Battle of Lincoln Fair

The final showdown with the rebel barons and the French invaders took place at the battle of Lincoln Fair on 20 May 1217. The English were led by William Longespée, William The Marshal Earl of Pembroke and his son William Marshal the Younger. The French and their allies were led by the Marshal of France the Count of Perche, a kinsman of William

Longespée. Lincoln Castle itself was still in the hands of that gallant royalist, Lady Nichola de la Haie, the Sheriff of Lincoln, wife of Gerard de Camville. She had succeeded her father, Baron de la Haie as hereditary castellan of the castle and had defended it from all attacks by the French and the English rebel barons. However most of the city itself was in the hands of the French and the rebels. Her leadership, knowledge of military tactics and her popularity among the rank and file of the castle's defenders was remarkable in a man's world.

Part of the French and rebel barons' army, led by Gilbert de Gant, had been besieging Lincoln Castle for some time. But they had failed to take it. Prince Louis then decided, in the Spring of 1217, to send his main forces, now liberally equipped with mangonells (military siege weapons used for throwing missiles at castle walls), to mount a sustained attack on the castle. Meanwhile, William The Marshal, the young King Henry III's Regent and Gualo, the Pope's Legate, convoked all available royalist forces to join up and raise the siege at Lincoln Castle. According to Roger of Wendover the chronicler, Gualo, having put on white robes, publicly excommunicated Prince Louis by name together with his French and English rebel leaders. He then pardoned the sins of all the members of the royalist army and promised them the reward of eternal salvation should they be killed in the forthcoming battle. This rhetoric inspired the royalists who immediately struck their camp, flew to arms, mounted their horses, and, loudly rejoicing, went into battle.

The royalist army then mounted its attack on the French and English rebel barons. Fawkes de Breaute, together with a large number of cross-bowmen, managed to find a safe way into the castle by a postern gate. They took up unassailable positions on the castle wall overlooking the rebels. As the main part of the royalist army attacked the city on a wide front, Fawkes' men opened a devastating fire on the crowded rebels below. This turned the fortunes of battle against the rebels, many of whose leaders had been killed, wounded, or captured, the rest lost heart and retreated headlong southwards leaving behind all their baggage trains.

According to *the Histoire*, William The Marshal saved Longespée's life just as he was about to be transfixed by Robert of Ropsley's lance. Roger of Wendover noted that the King's knights discovered and surrounded the Count of Perche in front of Lincoln Cathedral and called on him to surrender. But he said that he would not. Thereupon, an English knight rushed at him with a levelled lance, struck his eye through his helm and pierced his brain. The count died without uttering another word and was buried in the garden of the hospital outside the city. Unfortunately, for the citizens of Lincoln, the royalist army took their revenge on them by way of plunder and pillage 'to the last farthing' showing mercy to no-one: not even sparing the city's churches or the cathedral: thus earning the soubriquet 'The Fair'.

Meanwhile, news of the rebels' defeat spread far and wide and, as they fled towards London, they were ambushed by royal supporters while they passed through the towns and villages. On arrival at London they went before Prince Louis to tell him the sad news: in reply the French Prince sneered 'it is because you fled that your companions have been made prisoners. If you had stood firm, you would have saved yourselves and your companions from capture and death'. So that was how Prince Louis and the rebel English barons were soundly defeated on English soil seven months after the unexpected death of King John.

Later on the King's Council awarded Longespée the temporary custody of the castle and county of Lincoln; and the manors of Aldbourne and Wanborough in Wiltshire, previously the property of the unfortunate Count of Perche. William later adopted Wanborough as his chief seat in the shire.

William Longespée is Involved in a Second Great English Naval Victory

In August 1217 the French, directed from France by Prince Louis's wife Blanche, prepared to despatch strong reinforcements by sea to England in a fleet of eighty large ships and numerous smaller vessels, led by a notorious pirate, Eustace 'The Monk', by sea to Prince Louis. Hubert de Burgh, Justiciar to the King, who would become Regent of England on the death of William The Marshal, Earl of Pembroke, declared his intention to intercept these reinforcements at sea. But the royal generals replied 'We are not sailors, pirates or fishermen, do you therefore go and die'. Not so William Longespée, now reconciled once more with Hubert.

William Longespée collected the remains of the English fleet from the Cinque Ports, acquired reinforcements from the Dover garrison, obtained the blessing of the newly appointed Richard Poore, Bishop of Sarum, and joined Hubert. According to contemporary sources the small English fleet, comprising sixteen large ships and twenty small vessels, discovered the French fleet sailing before a fresh breeze straight for the North Foreland. The English steered an alternative course as though making for Calais which encouraged Eustace into thinking that so small a force would not dare to attack him.

Suddenly, as soon as the English were well to windward, they altered course and bore down on the rear ships of their enemy, pouring showers of arrows into the crowded transports. They boarded some and rammed others, overpowering each group one after another. A few French ships managed to escape, fifty seven were taken and the rest were sunk. Eustace, 'The Monk', was located, disguised and distraught, hiding in the bowels of his ship whence he was dragged out and beheaded. Surviving nobles and knights were spared and held to ransom.

Thus, nearly eight hundred years ago, on 24 August 1217 (St Bartholomew's Day), a small English fleet outsailed the pride of the French navy winning a great victory at sea so putting an end, once again, to French invasion plans.

Having Been Defeated Prince Louis Returns to France 'In all Honour'

Military activities came to an end on 20 September 1217 at the Peace of Lambeth. William Longespée and William The Marshal were closely involved with the peace negotiations and were witnesses at the signing of the Treaty. Prince Louis was given an indemnity of 10,000 marks, and the remains of his army were allowed to return to France with honour and his supporters were dealt with leniently. William The Marshal was much criticised by his contemporaries for his leniency to the French. However, David Crouch, historian, suggests that The Marshal may have calculated that England needed peace at this time more than anything else. But the Pope could not forgive the clergy involved and Elias de Dereham went into exile for two years.

Chapter Five

Earl William Longespée's Last Years. His Political Loyalties and Conflicting Personal Interests. His Final Campaign in France. His Delayed Return Home. Trouble at the Castle. His Death in 1226. Funeral and Epitaphs. Countess Ela's Life as a Widow for 35 Years. She Founds Lacock Abbey and becomes its Holy Abbess and Dies in 1261 aged 70. Three Famous Longspee Contemporaries – William The Marshal, Earl of Pembroke (The Elder), Regent of England and a Longespée Kinsman; Hubert de Burgh, Earl of Kent and Justiciar of England; and Peter des Roches, Bishop of Winchester.

Julia Boorman points out 'from 1217 until his death in 1226 the Earl of Salisbury enjoyed a position of considerable power, his career epitomizing both the centrifugal and the centripetal forces (outward and inward pressures on him) which so characterized the minority of Henry III. Within his areas of influence, he sought to exercise effective local autonomy without the interferences of central government. Between March 1217 and 1219 he had to make effective the grants of the lordship of Somerset and Dorset and, later, of Alnwick, extorted from the Regency, but failed against the continuing power of King John's sheriffs. He made repeated efforts to secure Lincoln Castle from the redoubtable Nicola de la Haie, the hereditary castellan claiming both custody of the castle and wardship of the rich Haie barony in Lincolnshire because his eldest son, still a minor, was betrothed to Idonea, daughter and heir of Richard de Camville (d. 1217). In May 1220, on the death of Robert of Berkeley, Salisbury seized Berkeley Castle and Robert's lands and chattels in a pre-emptive bid for wardship of his heir, 'against justice, the custom of the kingdoms and the law of the land', as the Earl of Pembroke complained to the Justiciar, Hubert de Burgh *(Shirley, no. clv, p.179)*'.

Julia Boorman continues 'Salisbury, nevertheless, professed himself strongly committed to government by the King's Council, stating forcefully in 1220 that the only legitimate orders were those sanctioned by the magnates of England who are held to be and are of the chief council of the King, with other chief men (Carpenter, 204). He supported the king and the Justiciar Hubert de Burgh at crucial moments in the restoration of royal authority. At Christmas 1221, and again at Northampton in December 1223, when the country came to the verge of civil war, he stood with the Justiciar against the powerful dissident faction of the Earl of Chester, Fawkes de Breaute, Engelard de Cigogne, Brian de Lisle and other castellans reluctant to yield up their shrievalties and castles'. In this, Salisbury represented in his own words, 'we native-born men of England (are) against those aliens who (we feel could be fermenting war within the kingdom) *(Shirley, no.CXCVI, p.221)*. In June 1222, on King Henry's second Act of Resumption of Royal Demesnes, he yielded a number of royal manors, and in February 1223 he surrendered Sarum Castle, only to receive it back directly, together with the custody of Shrewsbury and Bridgnorth castles, and the shrievalties of Shropshire and Staffordshire. Earl William continued to retain his role as a leading military commander until his death in 1226'.

William Longespée's Last Campaign in France and His Delayed Return Home

On 3 March 1225, Palm Sunday, William Longespée, together with his 16 year old Royal nephew, Richard Earl of Cornwall (to whom William had just been appointed military adviser) embarked for Gascony to hold the province against the King of France. Following the signing of a favourable treaty in November, William fell sick and decided to return home by sea. But violent gales drove the ship about for several days. All hope of safety was abandoned and his treasures and goods were cast overboard. Mathew Paris relates that, when the danger was at its height, a great light and a vision of the Blessed Virgin appeared at the masthead.

Soon afterwards the ship was driven ashore on the Island of Ré, off the present day port of La Rochelle on the west coast of France, which was held by Savaric de Mauleon (a French Poitevin mercenary leader who actively supported King John in England during the civil war; now enjoying a modus vivendi with the King of France on his French estate. He was also one of King John's executors and would have known William). The Earl of Salisbury and his men landed and took shelter in a Cistercian Abbey (identified as that of Notre Dame de Ré), pending favourable weather. After three days two of Savaric's officers, who knew him well, spoke to William privately and warned him that, unless he left before daylight the next day, he would be taken prisoner. Thereupon, William Longespée hastily collected his men and re-embarked in a great storm. They were tossed around the sea for many days before landing safely in Cornwall in early January 1226. On returning to Wiltshire, he was received with great rejoicing in Sarum Cathedral.

Meanwhile it was reported to Henry III that his uncle had been lost at sea. As soon as the courtiers heard this, Hubert de Burgh, still acting as Regent and in good faith, asked the king to allow his nephew, Raymond, to marry the Countess Ela. The king agreed on condition that the Countess herself should consent (a clause of Magna Carta stated that widows could no longer be forced to marry). When Raymond, 'all dressed up in knightly fashion', pressed his suit before the countess, she, with great anger, replied that she had received letters confirming her husband was safe and well; adding that, even if he were dead, she was too noble to marry a man of his rank. 'Seek elsewhere for a wife', she said, 'Because you will find from experience that you have come here to no purpose'. Whereupon Raymond returned home much disappointed and in some confusion.

The 13th century chronicler Wendover notes that, later, the king favoured Raymond by permitting him to marry Christina, the widow of William Manderville Earl of Essex, and gave him the castles of Berkhamstead and Hertford. Unfortunately, soon after, Raymond de Burgh was drowned in the River Loire in 1231 whilst serving with the English army in France.

There are very few historical references in contemporary accounts to indicate personal relationships between William and his beloved wife Ela. But the ups and downs of their lives indicate an unusually strong bonding between them. Despite William's many long absences abroad in the service of his monarch, Ela had eight children of whom seven grew to adulthood. She was clearly a pious woman according to many independent contemporary sources. She also managed to run a busy household in difficult conditions on top of the hill at Sarum. Of course life was not that bad, she came from a noble family with plenty of money, estates and had many friends and relatives living round about.

Moreover Ela was also responsible for running her husband's estates, dealing with legal problems and keeping a watchful eye on the garrison soldiers and their treatment of civilian neighbours and the clergy next door. She also carried out a great deal of charitable work over a wide area of Wiltshire. The nearby royal palace at Clarendon, recently enlarged and refurbished by Henry III, would have provided attractive breaks for her family and for pleasure-seeking friends and relatives. Also visits to the New Forest and other nearby royal forests would have been much enjoyed.

Their religion meant a great deal to both of them. This is revealed, firstly, by the unidentified Pontigny monk who, in his biography of Edmund Rich, Canon Treasurer of Sarum Cathedral 1222-30 (later Archbishop of Canterbury and canonised as St Edmund of

Abingdon) notes 'Ela was most distressed by William Longespée's failure to attend confession or take communion. Perceiving her husband to be imperilling his immortal soul, she urged him to avail himself of Edmund's spiritual counsel. The earl was deeply impressed by St. Edmund's holiness and, moved by reproaches and prayers of his wife, soon returned to his religious duties'. Secondly, Roger of Wendover says that William Longespée had a strong attachment to the Virgin Mary; and, since the day of his knighthood, he had kept a candle burning before her altar. In his will William gave generously to over twenty religious foundations.

William's Illness, Death, Funeral and Some Epitaphs

After William's return to the castle at Sarum, Ela related to him Raymond's approach to her. Much incensed William sought out the king, who was recovering from an illness in Marlborough, and complained bitterly of de Burgh's conduct in sending Raymond to woo his wife whilst he was still alive. De Burgh, who was present, immediately confessed his error and made up the quarrel by presents of horses and other valuable gifts and invited the earl to a banquet at his house. Soon afterwards William became seriously ill and retired to the castle at Sarum where he died on 7 March 1226. There was much talk in court and countryside suggesting that the de Burgh family had poisoned William. But it was well known that de Burgh and William were, by then, close friends; and the ODNB states that this story is undoubtedly false.

When William Longespée's tomb was opened centuries later, a dead rat was found in his skull. The rat's state of preservation indicated that it may have died from arsenic poisoning. However it is much more likely that William died from an accumulation of medical problems brought on by the physical and mental stress of a remarkably active life. It may be worth noting that balm used on wounds at that time often contained a little arsenic, so it may be that traces of arsenic, which had come from that source, had been absorbed in William's body over a long period and the rat might well have died from over-indulgence.

The magnificent tomb of William Longspée, third Earl of Salisbury in Salisbury Cathedral. Born c. 1160, died 1226.

Shortly before his death, William Longespée is said to have sent for the Bishop of Salisbury, Richard Poore. On his arrival, William dragged himself from his bed, stripped, thrust a rope around his neck and cried out that he had been a traitor to God and begged the Bishop's forgiveness. Perhaps he had in mind his own cruelty in battle, especially during and after the ravages of Ely and the battles round Lincoln. He refused to rise until he had made his confession and received the sacrament. His bier was carried from the castle at Sarum to the new, largely incomplete, cathedral in a torchlight procession, through a flurry of wind and rain. An onlooker at his funeral noted that his salvation was betokened by the fact that the tapers accompanying his funeral procession from the castle to the cathedral remained alight despite the inclement weather. Countess Ela performed homage to the king for her inheritance twelve days later. But she was required to surrender Sarum Castle back to the king.

He was interred in the recently completed Trinity Chapel and was the first person to be buried in the cathedral. His funeral was attended by Richard Poore the Bishop of Salisbury; Peter des Roches the very powerful Bishop of Winchester, who, three years later, was to play a constructive part in the Sixth Crusade which recaptured Jerusalem in 1229; several bishops from Ireland; William Marshal the Younger (Earl of Pembroke); Earl William de Mandeville and three Barons, all with a great multitude of their military attendants.

His tomb was moved in the late 18th century by the architect-restorer, James Wyatt, to the north side of the south aisle, where it is greatly distinguished by the survival of its extremely rare painted oak base remarkable for its colouring and inlay on gesso. His shield shows the six golden lioncels proclaiming his ancestry. Ben Elliott, historian (heraldry) and Cathedral Guide, notes that this is one of the very earliest recorded examples of the transmission of a coat of arms in this country.

Professor Kemp has this to say of William Longespée's tomb chest:

'Salisbury has what is probably the earliest identified military effigy in England... examination of his arcaded memorial shows he is at rest and relaxed. He wears a coat of mail from head to foot with a surcoat on top. His elbows and knees are unprotected. There is a lovely trail of beautifully carved foliage around the slab with a cushion to support his feet. Originally all would have been painted, so that only a close inspection would reveal the details of stone and wood – it would have appeared all in one from a distance'.

The ODNB includes this epitaph for William Longespée, 3rd Earl of Salisbury. 'He was a wise and valiant man, not indeed to be ranked with patriot statesmen, such as William The Earl Marshal or Hubert de Burgh. But far superior to most of the nobles of his day and sincerely attached to the interests of the Royal House from which he came; faithful as long as it was possible to his brother John and a good servant to his young nephew Henry. He seems to have been hot-tempered; but, though concerned during the war between John and the barons in some cruel ravages, was religious and has the good word of the monastic chroniclers'.

Mathew Paris, the chronicler, sums up with this epitaph, which freely translated from the Latin reads:

'When William, Flower of the Earls, resigned
His princely breath
His long sword was content to find
A shorter sheath'.

In the History of Pembroke, Meyer quotes the following contemporary epitaph for William 'He was a loyal, courageous and skilful commander, whose mother was largesse and whose banner was powerfulness' (Meyer II, 12125-8) the former compliment, perhaps, being a tactful inversion of his illegitimacy.

For Notes on William The Marshal, Earl of Pembroke, and Hubert de Burgh, and Peter des Roches please see pages 49-56.

The seal of the Countess Ela, High Abbess of Lacock Abbey c. 1240.

The seal of Salisbury Cathedral.

Countess Ela Longespée's Later Life as Founder and Holy Abbess of Lacock Abbey

At the time of her husband's death Ela had seven surviving children between the ages of four and sixteen. On 14 September 1227 she honoured her husband's memory by giving land in the parish of West Dean to St Nicholas' Hospital (in Salisbury) as well as many animals to graze upon the donated pastures.

Also in 1227 Countess Ela exercised her personal right to become the Sheriff of Wiltshire thus becoming the first lady Sheriff of the county. She held this appointment in 1227-8 and again from 1231-1237. This office had also been held by her husband, father and grandfather although a subsequent case in the king's court made it clear that she had no heritable right to the shrievalty. Acting on the advice of Edmund Rich, Canon Treasurer of Salisbury Cathedral, she began the process of obtaining permission to establish a religious house in a meadow called Snailsmead on her manor at Lacock in Wiltshire. This village is mentioned in the Domesday Book as belonging to Edward, Sheriff of Wiltshire, who was Countess Ela's great great grandfather. In 1230 Countess Ela was instructed by King Henry III to surrender all the lands, which she held by inheritance from her husband, to her eldest son William Longespée II in satisfaction of his claim to them. On 16 April 1232 she laid the foundation stone of her abbey for Augustinian canonesses dedicating it to St Mary and St Bernard (now a National Trust property). On the same day she rode off to her park at Hinton, fifteen miles away to the south of Bath, and rededicated a Charterhouse for Carthusian monks, originally founded by her late husband in Hatherop, and then rode back to Lacock.

In 1237 she gave up much of her secular life and passed the custody of the royal castle at Sarum to her eldest son. Two years later the Abbey was completed and upgraded from a priory to an abbey. She then took the veil and was elected its Holy Abbess and, according to a local scribe, 'ruled her house with diligence and more than female vigour'. The abbey estate had been richly endowed by Ela and was financed by revenue from the production of wool, corn and hides from its surrounding farms. The nuns were mostly ladies of good family numbering about twenty five. Two of her great grand-daughters, Lorica and Katherine, became nuns at Lacock, and two of her sons (Richard and Stephen), and great great grand-daughter Margaret (de Laci) were buried in the Abbey. There were also up to twenty young girl boarders who were admitted when their parents were away from home (perhaps they were visiting relatives in France).

This religious community was served by lay sisters and the outside world would have been represented by a constant flow of estate workers, travellers and guests. The Holy Abbess Ela retired from old age in 1257 and died there on 24 August 1261 at the age of seventy having been a widow for thirty five years. She was buried in the choir of the Abbey church which is no longer in existence. Her declaration of canonical obedience, small, signed with a cross and addressed to the Bishop of Salisbury, is in the Salisbury Chapter archives and is sometimes on display in Salisbury Cathedral Chapter House.

After flourishing for 307 years Lacock Abbey was suppressed by King Henry VIII in 1539. The property reverted to the crown and was sold to Sir William

Lacock Abbey Cloisters.

Sharrington for £783.13.10. He converted the Abbey into a large comfortable private mansion. More alterations were made by subsequent owners and much of the building which would have been known to Ela, has disappeared. But, with imagination, the cold dormitories of the Augustinian canonesses may still be discovered, as can a stone spiral staircase, used regularly by Ela, when going from her private lodgings into the cloister. Her doorway into the church is now a window. Half way up the nearby staircase there is a squint through which she could have watched the nuns ambling round the cloister.

The tomb slab in the cloister, within the iron railings, is said to be that of Ela, having been moved from her original burial place. Its translated Latin inscription reads *'Below lie the bones of the venerable Ela, who gave this sacred house as a home for the nuns. She also lived here as the Holy Abbess and Countess of Salisbury, famous for her good works'*. It is frustrating to note that this inscription is very likely to have been inscribed in the 18th century. Among the Abbey's treasures is a good example of Ela's great seal depicting the six Longespée lioncels and a standing female figure with long tresses, one hand placed on her heart, the other holding a hawk. John of Salisbury, who became Bishop of Chartres, is said to have observed that women were better at hawking than men because the worst people were always the most predatory. Her heir on her death was her great-granddaughter Margaret Longespée who married Henry de Laci, Earl of Lincoln.

The suppression came soon after an inspection by the King's Commissioners who found the Abbey 'in no disorder'. As in many other religious institutions, the Holy Abbess Ela had dedicated her foundation at Lacock to the souls of her husband, his ancestors and to the souls of her family and their ancestors. Thus, this dedication contained the seeds of its eventual destruction – because prayers for the dead, the belief in purgatory and plenary indulgences were abolished by Luther and the newly promulgated Protestant religion in England (Catholic but reformed, Protestant and Church of England) - and replaced by a simple definition of personal faith and belief in the Grace of God. Consequently, Lacock Abbey was suppressed for this reason and, more importantly perhaps, other more secular (ie royal financial) reasons.

Three Famous Longspée Contemporaries

1. William The Marshal, Earl of Pembroke, Regent of England and a Longespée Kinsman

2. Hubert de Burgh, Earl of Kent and Justiciar of England, and

3. Peter des Roches, Bishop of Winchester, Crusader and Pilgrim

A quote from William Shakespeare's King John Act IV, Scene III

(Earl William Longespée (wrongly) suspects that Hubert de Burgh has murdered the king's nephew, Prince Arthur, by putting out his eyes).

Earl of Salisbury (Longespée)	*'Avaunt, thou hateful villain, get thee hence'*
Hubert de Burgh	*'I am no villain'*
Longespée (drawing his sword)	*'Must I rob the law?'*
Bastard (to Longespée)	*'Your sword is bright, Sir, put it up again'*
Longespée	*'Not till I sheathe it in a murderer's skin'*
Earl of Pembroke	*'Cut him to pieces, William'*
Hubert de Burgh	*'Stand back, my lord, stand back, I say; by Heaven I think my sword's as sharp as yours"*

No account of the Longespée family should ignore the part played by the following three outstanding leaders in those momentous days. They dominated the English stage throughout the last quarter of the 12th century and the early years of the 13th century. They must have been ever-present in the thoughts of William Longespée, Earl of Salisbury.

1. William Marshal, Earl of Pembroke (c. 1146-1219)

Historians Julia Boorman and David Crouch state (in summary) 'the word Marshal comes from the Frankish words li Mareschal meaning horse-slave and likely to have originated from the word applied to the unfree grooms of the ancestors of the Merovingian kings of the Franks (Frank. A member of the Germanic nation or nations that conquered Gaul in the 6th century and from which the country received the name France. Also, in the Eastern Mediterranean region – a person of Western nationality. OERD). From then on the name Marshal continued via the Carolingan courts, to the courts of the kings of France. The

Normans brought the word to England. According to the *Constitutio Domus Regis* (the Organisation of the King's Household) dated 1136, the English court then had a Master Marshal, namely John (William Marshal's father), which ranked him with the other great officers such as the seneschal, the constable and the master chamberlain. In William Marshal's case, he would have acquired his surname from the occupation of his father, and not from his promotion to the rank of Earl Marshal (much later) in the king's court'.

Left: William Marshall, the Elder, 1st Earl of Pembroke (New Creation) c. 1146 - 1219 *Right:* William The Marshall, the Younger, 2nd Earl of Pembroke d. 1213. Both photos taken in the V&A's Cast Court.

John Marshal (d. 1165) was the son of Gilbert Marshal in the court of Henry I. He features by name as master marshal in the *Constitutio* and, at first, was a supporter of *King Stephen* after the death of Henry I and accompanied him on his Norman tour of 1137. According to the annals of Winchester he garrisoned the castle of Marlborough and Ludgershall on the king's behalf. But, later, he changed sides and supported Empress Matilda. After the capture of Stephen at Lincoln in February 1141, John remained firmly committed to the Empress's cause, and William Gifford, his brother, became the Empress's chancellor. The Histoire preserves a number of stories of local warfare between John and Earl Patrick d'Evreux. As already seen, this family quarrel was resolved when John Marshal agreed to divorce his first wife, Adelina, and married (c. 1145) the Earl's sister, Sybil, daughter of Walter of Salisbury.

See Pembroke family tree on page 145.

William The Marshal was probably born in Wiltshire in 1146 or early 1147, the fourth son of John Marshal and Sybil, sister of Earl Patrick D'Evreux. In 1152, during the civil war between King Stephen and the Empress Matilda, John Marshal, supporting the Empress, offered William, then aged five or six, as a pledge for a truce with King Stephen who was blockading John Marshal's new castle near Newbury. But John Marshal, reckless of his son's life, used the truce to provision the castle instead. When challenged by King Stephen that his son would die as a result, John Marshal is said to have uttered the notorious response 'I do not care about the child, since I still have the anvils and hammers to produce even finer ones'. The king made several attempts to convince the indifferent garrison that he would execute the boy but did not, in the end, permit it. William seems to have remained at court, more as the king's ward than a captive, until November 1153. John Marshal became prominent in Henry II's court and was allowed to keep most of his gains from Stephen's reign. But his fortunes gradually declined and he died in 1165. He was succeeded by his son John Marshal who was left the entire estate and the office of Marshal. John died in 1194 and was succeeded by his younger brother William The Marshal. He spent the rest of his youth fostered into the household of a relation, William de Tankarville, Royal Chamberlain of Normandy, who was his mother's cousin.

William, now a squire in the household, was knighted by William de Tankarville in 1166. Later on, during his first pitched battle in France, de Tankarville rebuked William for being too forward in the action; 'Get back, William' he shouted 'Don't be such a hothead, let the knights through!' But he continued to distinguish himself in the skirmish. Shortly after he lost his horse in the cut and thrust of a street fight in the suburbs of Neufchatel and failed to take advantage of an opportunity to seize the ransoms that would have retrieved the situation. This was ironically pointed out to him by the Earl of Essex who, at the victory banquet, asked him loudly for various items of saddlery and harness which he could not produce; but of which he could have had his pick, had he fought professionally, rather than boyishly.

In 1168, he was captured by the Lusignans *(see page 26)*. After his release he joined the household of young Prince Henry, also known as 'the Young King', Henry II's second son. William The Marshal soon became famous for his physical strength, skill and successes on the tournament fields of Normandy and England from which he received enough financial reward to defray the costs of raising his own banner at the great tournament at Lagny-sur-Marne in 1180.

On Prince Henry's untimely death, near Limoges in 1183 from a fever whilst leading rebels against his royal father, William took ship for the Holy Land, having vowed to take over Prince Henry's personal cloak and Cross. He stayed two years fighting for King Guy of Jerusalem and the Knights Templar. On his return to England in 1186, Henry II gave him the fief (feudal estate) of Cartmel in Cumbria; and he served his monarch as royal adviser and ambassador gaining a reputation as an astute diplomat and earning his monarch's respect and affection.

On 12th June 1189, whilst fighting for Henry II in France, he encountered the king's son, Prince Richard (The Lionheart), riding lightly armed, well ahead of his troops in active revolt against his father 'By God's legs, William, do not kill me' shouted Richard 'I have no hauberk'. Replied William 'may the devil kill you, for I shall not be the one to do it' and, thrusting his lance into Richard's horse, killed it, unseating Richard. Then he cantered off to warn the king (who died less than a month later) to avoid direct confrontation with his son.

Shortly after this incident Richard The Lionheart succeeded his father as King and he gave William, a relatively poor knight without great estates and retainers, the hand in marriage of Isabel de Clare, sole heiress of the late Richard de Clare (Strongbow d. 1176), the 2nd Earl of Pembroke (First Creation) and succeeded him as Earl of Pembroke (Second Creation), and of his wife Aoife, daughter of Dermot McMurrough, King of Leinster. Thus, William not only acquired all his bride's extensive lands becoming one of the king's richest subjects; but also received half the Giffard Estates (including Caversham), the Shrievalty (Sheriff) of Gloucester, the keeping of the Forest of Dean and much land in Ireland. He carried a sword of state at King Richard's solemn crownwearing at Winchester on 17 April 1194.

While King Richard was dying in Chinon castle, near Tours, from a shoulder wound on 6 April 1199, the Marshal was at Vaudreuil acting as a ducal justice. Whilst there he heard the news of the king's injury and received a royal writ directing him to take charge of the Tower of Rouen and to secure that city. He heard of the king's death three days later while on the point of going to bed. He crossed the city in the night to discuss the Royal succession with Archbishop Hubert Walter. William declared himself a supporter of Count John for the succession, rather than the king's nephew, Arthur of Brittany, 'since the son is indisputably closer in the line of inheritance than the nephew is'. Whereupon the Archbishop warned William saying 'you will never come to regret anything you did as much as what you are doing now' (*History, II. II900-6*). The Marshal went to England to urge his fellow magnates to support John. He then returned to Normandy and joined John's household as it prepared to make the Channel crossing immediately before John's coronation (27 May 1199).

William Marshal maintained the place at the royal court he had held under King Richard in King John's first years and certainly found little cause at this time to regret his choice in 1199 whatever the Archbishop of Canterbury is alleged to have warned. He had reached a peak of personal influence and power by 1201 being very close to the new king's council. But his career slowly became tainted by the king's failure to maintain his (military) position in northern France. The Marshal had been detailed from 1201 onwards to protect Upper Normandy but his efforts were increasingly compromised by the king's political misjudgements. In December 1203 the Marshal accompanied the king on his departure from Normandy for England after which the duchy fell rapidly to the French invaders.

William was an outstanding commander of the army in northern France. For example, he played a particularly courageous part in the taking of the castle at Milly-sur-Therain, near Beauvais, in 1198, when he climbed a scaling-ladder and defended a section of the wall. At that time he was over fifty years of age; but age had not wearied him enough to prevent him flattening the Constable of Milly when he met him on the wall walk. However the chronicler reports that the breathless Earl had to sit down on the Constable's unconscious body to get his breath back.

Having been involved in the loss of Normandy to King Philip II of France; William Marshal, Earl of Pembroke, suffered serious personal losses of land. Subsequent disagreements with

King John over his plans to recover his losses, together with William's refusal to accompany the king to Poitou, caused a serious break in their friendship. Eventually, this ended up in 1204 by John calling William a traitor, and William's decision to retire into the political wilderness of rural Ireland for several years. In 1212 a thaw in their relationship developed and, in 1213, William was recalled to the Court and many of his former possessions and responsibilities were returned to him. Following the disaster at the battle of Bouvines in 1214 William reverted to his old style of 'middle-road' politics in John's quarrel with the rebelling barons but loyally supported King John throughout the civil war.

William Marshal continued to support the royal cause, mainly in Wales, until King John's sudden death in October 1216. He was an executor of John's will and took responsibility for the staging of his funeral. He convened a Council at Gloucester to ratify the arrangements for a Protectorship of the State (Regency) and took over the 'Guardianship of the boy-king Henry III – becoming Rector of his Kingdom' and affixed his seal as Earl of Pembroke on the relevant documents. He also kept in close contact with the Papal legate, whose presence lent him moral authority and legitimacy.

In 1217 he led the royalist troops which took Mountsorrel castle in Leicestershire and then played a significant part in the battle of Lincoln Fair leading a powerful loyalist column against his first cousin, the French commander, Count of Perche. William rode into the battle accompanied by his son. An observer noted 'so keen for battle was the Earl, that a page noticed and reminded him that he had not put on his helm'. The Marshal, now aged seventy two, engaged in personal combat in the streets of Lincoln, using his weight and skill as a horseman, to force himself deep into the enemy ranks. During the fighting under the west towers of the cathedral he struck down Robert of Ropsley who, himself, had just unseated William Longespée, the Earl of Salisbury. Then, suddenly and sadly, William Marshal's eye caught sight of the Count of Perche in the moment of his death as he was struck by a sword penetrating through the eyehole of his helm.

William Marshal was the chief negotiator at the Treaty of Lambeth in 1217, which restored peace and order in England, and treated Prince Louis and the rebel barons leniently, wisely and fairly. Two months or so later, suspecting his death was upon him, quotes David Crouch 'he was rowed up the Thames to his home in Caversham, near Reading, and there, for a while, carried on as the country's Regent. Meanwhile, the boy king was brought to Reading with his tutor, the Bishop of Winchester. At a council held in the sick-chamber on 8th and 9th April 1219 he relinquished power to the Pope's legate' (England was still a vassal of the Pope), thus snubbing the pretensions of Bishop Peter des Roches of Winchester. He died on 14 May 1219. His repaired effigy is in the Temple Church in London – a plaster cast, taken before the Temple Church was bombed by the Luftwaffe in 1941, is usually on display in the cast court department of the Victoria and Albert Museum, London.

Mathew Paris, the contemporary chronicler, describes William The Marshal Earl of Pembroke, as 'a figure of some ambiguity, too easy on the French and too harsh on the church'. Later historians saw him as the chivalric hero of his day quoting King Philip II of France's words 'the best knight in all the world'. The ODNB says of him 'in fact the Marshal was a military captain of some international repute, and a physically accomplished sportsman and warrior. Principally, he was a courtier and trained to be such from boyhood. He cultivated and practised carefully the differential and affable behaviour necessary for survival in the retinues of greater men. He was in his mid-forties before he was placed into any situation where a broader, political judgement was needed. It was consistent misjudgement in pursuing his own interests that brought The Marshal down in 1205. His tired decision to retreat into self-imposed exile in 1206 should have been the end of his active career. But King John's own difficulties, The Marshal's undeserved reputation for political wisdom, and his deserved reputation for military success, pulled him out of retirement. His luck was that he was the ideal man for the moment in 1216. Perhaps, too, by this time, his great age made it easier for him to command obedience and respect'.

His wife Isobel died a year after William. They had five sons and five daughters. But the Marshal line became extinct in 1245.

A simplified family tree of William, Earl of Pembroke, showing his relationship with the Longespée family is attached on page 145.

William The Marshal's eldest son, William (the Younger) received the earldom and the bulk of his father's lands in England, Wales and Ireland; Richard, his second son, received the Norman lands and the Gifford manors in England; Gilbert, his third son, became a simple clerk; his fourth son Walter's share included many manors in England and Goodrich Castle in Wales. His fifth son, Anselm, was left a large sum of cash. He left his body to the Temple Church in London having obtained a plenary indulgence for his sins.

2. Hubert de Burgh, Earl of Kent (1170-1243)

He was born into a minor land-owning Norfolk family. As a young man he joined his brother in the household of King John and became its Chamberlain. In 1200 the king made him custodian of Windsor and Dover royal castles. In 1201 he was Sheriff of Dorset and Somerset and, next year, of Berkshire and Cornwall. In 1203 he was made custodian of the Welsh Marches and head of one hundred men-at-arms; and given the Welsh castles of Grosmont, Skenfreth and Whitecastle. The king also gave him further manors, baronies and many grants – so much so that Hubert became a significant and powerful figure in the land.

Suddenly, in 1202, he was summoned to France, where rebel barons and the French were attacking English possessions, and was appointed Constable of Falaise Castle in Normandy; and also joint castellan of Chinon in Touraine (it was at Falaise that Hubert de Burgh refused to blind - and castrate - Prince Arthur, not at Northampton Castle as dramatically described by Shakespeare in his play King John, quoted earlier in this Chapter). His task was to defend the area from an imminent siege by the French. Eventually, after a year of this siege, the walls of Chinon were breached: whereupon the English garrison rushed out to engage the French in a fierce fight during which Hubert was wounded and captured. He was a prisoner of the French for two years and was compelled to forfeit most of his 'royal' possessions in England. However King John helped with the ransom money and Hubert was released in 1207 and returned home. He soon recovered most of the land he had lost and in 1209 married Beatrice de Warenne, who died in 1214 having borne him his only son, John. He continued to serve his monarch in England and France acquiring yet more property, baronies and a great deal of money. He was appointed deputy, then proclaimed Seneschal, of Poitou from 1212-1215. After the battle of Bouvines in 1214 he was one of the witnesses to the truce by which King John retained his lands in France south of the river Loire.

Immediately after Magna Carta was sealed in 1215 Hubert de Burgh was appointed Chief Justiciar and played an important political and military part during the civil war, as already described, basing himself on the royal castle of Dover. In 1217 Hubert married the late King John's divorced wife Queen Isabella, the Countess of Gloucester. She died a few days after the wedding ceremony. In 1217 he was re-appointed Justiciar and stayed in post until 1224. In 1223 there was a general surrender of all the royal castles for redistribution by the king. De Burgh handed over those at Canterbury, Dover, Rochester, Norwich, Oxford and

Hereford to the bishops of those places; as a result of this he gained the political support of the Archbishop of Canterbury. The castles held as part of his shrievalities were handed back to the king during the re-establishment of royal government.

In 1223 de Burgh and the young Henry III completed a successful expedition against the Welsh. However, subsequent expeditions into Wales were not so successful and this annoyed the king. Nevertheless he granted the Justiciarship to Hubert for life and arranged for him to receive back his custodianship of the royal castles at Dover, Canterbury and Rochester and, also, the Welsh castles of Montgomery, Cardigan and Carmarthen.

In 1225 he accompanied Henry III on a formal visit to New Sarum and presented a gold text Bible to Bishop Richard Poore.

During his last years of office Hubert de Burgh continued to lose the confidence and support of his monarch. His latest military operations had proved unsuccessful e.g. the Welsh expeditions of 1228 and 1231 and the loss of more land in France. Moreover his administration of the great offices of State, and his ability to raise sufficient money for royal expenses, had waned.

In 1232 Peter de Roches, Bishop of Winchester and energetic politician, persuaded the king to dismiss and imprison Hubert. But Hubert escaped dramatically in 1233 and achieved a reconciliation with the king a year later. However he never recovered his former position and influence.

Hubert de Burgh died in May 1243 at his Surrey manor of Banstead and was buried in the House of the Blackfriars at Westminster. Countess Margaret, sister of King Alexander II of Scotland, whom he had married in 1221, died in 1259 without issue.

The ODNB has this to say of Hubert de Burgh; 'his career clearly shows the great rewards faithful royal service could bring to a man of minor land-holding origins, and 'loyal' or 'constant' have been words applied to him by scholars. What is remarkable, is that his loyal service did not make him unacceptable to the baronial opposition to John, and that he was able to serve Henry III within the limits set to royal government by Magna Carta. He was also seen to be as 'English' in his patriotic opposition to the arbitrary excesses of 'foreigners' (ie the Poitevins). Contemporary hostility to Hubert de Burgh can be accounted for by resentment of his, and his family's, great acquisitiveness in office; but even more by the loss of the king's favour; both through military failure at the end of his life and through the growth of specialised branches of royal administration, which made effective control by a single great minister impossible. Hubert de Burgh was the last of the great Judiciars'.

3. Peter des Roches, Bishop of Winchester, Courtier, Politician, Judiciar of England, Pilgrim, Crusader and Military Leader (c. 1175-1238)

Peter was born in Touraine, NW France. He entered the service of the Angevin kings in 1197. He left France c. 1203, after the French had overrun Normandy, and came to England where he was appointed financial controller of King John's household. He worked diligently and won the confidence and friendship of his monarch. In 1204 King John proposed him for the vacant See at Winchester. But the Archdeacon of Winchester and Surrey strongly opposed this appointment, much preferring the candidature of Richard Poore, then Dean of the cathedral at Old Sarum, and the illegitimate son of a former Bishop of Winchester (Richard of Ilchester).

However the Pope approved the appointment of des Roches, aged thirty, on 25 September 1205. Although, supposedly owing allegiance to the Pope in Rome, he was one of two bishops who remained loyal to King John throughout the royal quarrel with the Papacy. He was the king's Justiciar from 1213-15. On John's death in 1216 he was appointed one of his executors and a Guardian of the young King Henry III; thus becoming a powerful political figure in the early years of Henry's minority. However he was unpopular with local people who, it was said, referred to him as 'up at the Exchequer, keen on Finance, slack at Scripture'.

He was present at the sealing of Magna Carta in 1215 and supported the king during the early days of the civil war. He played a leading role at the coronation of King Henry III. Throughout this period he strongly promoted the interests of the king's mercenaries (the Poitevins) to whom he gave land, money and appointed many of these people to the highest offices in the kingdom. The battle of Lincoln cemented his military reputation. He commanded the royal bowmen and was responsible for enabling the royalist army to enter the city via a poorly blocked-up gate, taking many prisoners and enabling his men to relieve the castle – so ably defended for so long, against all odds, by its redoubtable hereditary castellan Dame Nicola de la Haie.

After leaving Lincoln (before the uncontrolled victory celebrations) he was one of the first royalists to storm into London and accept the rebel barons' surrender of the City at the Tower of London. In 1221 he went on a pilgrimage to Santiago de Compostella. In 1227 Peter took ship for the Holy Land and joined the English contingent in the Sixth Crusade. Once again he distinguished himself by his military expertise and, together with William, Bishop of Exeter, witnessed the Treaty by which the Saracens ceded the City of Jerusalem to the Crusaders. After spending two years or so in Rome he returned to England in 1232 and persuaded the king to arrest and dismiss Hubert de Burgh. Peter des Roches died at Farnham in 1238. His heart was taken to Waverley Abbey and his body was buried in Winchester Cathedral where his black marbled tomb may still be seen (2011) – unmarked, unrecognisable and lonely in its obscurity.

As Bishop of Winchester, Crusader to the Holy Land, pilgrim to Santiago, the founder of the re-organised militant Order of St Thomas in Acre and founder of a Cistercian House, he was certainly a religious man. He was also very generous to his friends and to religious orders in England and in France. His Episcopal household contained many poor scholars and priests including Master Elias de Derham (later the most respected Designer-Canon of the new cathedral at Salisbury). He gave at least one religious relic (the foot of St Philip) to the monks of Winchester Cathedral and also left them property and cash in perpetuity. This generosity did not prevent them from complaining that their bishop was 'as hard as rocks' (as a play on his name). However his life-style and his politics were never to the English taste and he was widely thought to be 'better versed in battle and how to lay siege to a castle; than preaching the word of God'. Certainly very powerful for most of his life, he was always considered by the populace as one of King John's cruel, merciless, unwelcome Poitevin foreigners.

Chapter Six

Background to the Holy Land Pilgrimages and Summaries of the Six Earlier Middle East Crusades. Muslim Reactions and Jihad (Personal Holy War). Saladin's Arrival on the Scene and His Death in 1188.

Readers may wonder why the next two chapters on the Crusades have been included in this book of which the main interests are Wessex, 'The Man Who Moved A Cathedral' and the amazing Longespée Family. The reason is that it is interesting to summarise the Crusades in the Middle East at this time and to note the effect on people living in the English countryside; and to relate the courageous and bloody death of the Earl of Salisbury's eldest son Sir William Longespée.

In the third Century AD the Holy Land became a magnet for Christian pilgrims from Constantinople and the West. It was much encouraged by the Byzantine Emperor Constantine whose wife, Helena, visited Palestine where she discovered Calvary and searched for holy relics. The Emperor was so impressed that he built the church of the Holy Sepulchre which soon became the greatest Holy Place of all. Pilgrims continued to arrive in great numbers and many famous people joined the stream, including St Jerome, who settled at Bethlehem taking with him, it is said, many fashionable and rich ladies. By the end of that century some two hundred Christian monasteries and hospices had been constructed around Jerusalem for the benefit of pilgrims.

Later, Count William I of Aquitaine founded the Abbey of Cluny which soon became the centre of organised pilgrimages to Muslim destinations in Spain and to the Holy Land. The number of pilgrims from Germany and Scandinavia increased too, especially when a new route was opened by land through Hungary, Belgrade, Sophia and Adrianople: with an alternative route through Italy, Bari to Dyrrhachium and Thessalonika to the Bosphorus and on to the ancient city of Antioch. These routes were cheaper, safer and easier than travelling by sea. Many countries continued to be avoided because of heavy local taxes. Constantinople was the largest and most populous city in Europe with a stable government, wonderful architecture, a shopping paradise and full of extremely expensive religious relics such as the Crown of Thorns (King Louis IX of France is said to have paid the equivalent today of £2,000,000 for the Crown); Christ's face imprinted on a cloth; the hair of St John the Baptist (a lock of which is said to have been taken to England and stored in Salisbury Cathedral whence it seems to have disappeared before or during the Reformation); the mantle of Elijah and the body parts of innumerable saints, prophets and martyrs. Nevertheless, the pilgrimages always had an element of danger and organisations, such as the Knights Templar and the Knights of St John, were extraordinarily successful, and popular too, in keeping pilgrims reasonably safe and well looked after (until, of course, the final withdrawal of these Knights from the Holy Land).

For an outline map of the eastern Mediterranean, please see inside back cover.

The First Crusade (1096-99) was launched with great panache by Pope Urban II and the first person to take the Cross was Adhemar of Monteil, Bishop of Le Puy. Its aim was to protect Latin Christendom (in the East Mediterranean) from incursions by the Seljuk Turks and other warlike Muslim factions intent on recapturing the Holy Places in Palestine and to ensure the safety of pilgrims travelling to the Holy Land. Despite incredible hardships the Crusaders' military operations were successfully accomplished. But their success brought with it fearful massacres of the civilian inhabitants of Jerusalem including the entire Muslim and Jewish communities. These massacres profoundly shocked the Western world and horrified local

Christians. 'So much so that, when Latin Christians of the Eastern Mediterranean sought to find some basis on which Christians and Muslims could live and work together, the memory of the massacres stood always in the way', says Sir Stephen Runciman in his *History of the Crusades*. Saladin, the capable commander of the Muslim armies, recaptured Jerusalem eighty eight years later on 2 October 1187. However the First Crusade established a strong Latin Christian presence along the eastern Mediterranean coast which lasted for about 150 years. Historian and author M.T. Clanchey says that at least eight of the leading generals of this Crusade were either Norman or had strong Norman connections and that among them were both a son and a son-in-law of William the Conqueror.

The Second Crusade (1147-49). Following its launch St Bernard, the famous and much respected Abbot of Clairvaux in France (1090-1153), in a letter to Pope Eugenius III on the effects of his preaching participation in this Crusade, wrote 'I spoke, and at once the Crusaders (from here) multiplied to infinity. Villages and towns are now deserted. You will scarcely find one man for every seven women. Everywhere you see widows whose husbands are still alive ...' As the Roman Catholic hymn says today

> *Follow me, follow me. Leave your home and family, leave your fishing nets and boats upon the shore. Leave the seed that you have sown. Leave the crops that you have grown. Leave the people you have known and follow me*.

The Crusade was led by King Louis VII of France and King Conrad III of Germany. The German contingent, ten thousand strong, left first and plundered their way across the Balkans looting, murdering, burning and raping without check; so much so that local people, much incensed, fell upon any stragglers they could find and butchered them in turn. On their arrival in the Holy Land they were attacked by waiting Muslim forces and some 90% of the Imperial Army were either killed, captured or wounded. It was a complete fiasco. Meanwhile the French Army marched through Germany, crossed the River Danube and on to Constantinople. Here a local chronicler noted

'some women travelling in the ranks of the Crusaders, boldly sit astride in their saddles as men do, dressed as men and armed with lances or battle-axes ... at their head one, in particular, was a richly dressed lady wearing gold embroidery on the hem of her dress. The elegance of her bearing and the freedom of her movement recalled to him Penthesilea, the celebrated leader of the Amazons'.

Eleanor of Aquitaine (c. 1122 - 1.204). The divorced wife of King Louis VII of France. Later married King Henry II of England. She almost certainly accompanied the Second Crusade as a female leader of the French Court. Effigy is at the V&A Museum Cast Court.

Alison Weir, historian, who wrote *'Eleanor of Aquitaine'*, suggests that this lady was almost certainly Eleanor herself, consort of King Louis VII of France who, later, married Henry II and was travelling in style accompanied by the ladies of the French court.

The French resumed their march towards the Holy Land and eventually caught up with the remnants of Emperor Conrad's army. Conrad himself had been severely wounded in the head and had to be sent back to Constantinople to recover. The

French continued their advance toward Antioch. Suddenly a strong force of Muslims attacked the Crusaders killing several thousands – King Louis' horse was killed under him. The Crusaders struggled on, half-starving with many suffering from the plague. The 'Amazons' lost all their belongings. Bishops, who had worn out their shoes, were walking on bare feet. Local food was expensive and scarce. A large number of German and French deserters were captured by the Muslims and, in order to save their lives, were forced to convert to Islam. After resting a while at Antioch King Louis decided to continue the march towards Jerusalem where the Crusaders arrived exhausted and demoralised.

After a short respite King Louis decided to mount an assault on the Muslim Emirate of Damascus. But, after a four days' siege of the city, the ill-prepared assault proved a humiliating failure and the Crusaders were forced to retreat with considerable loss of life. In Alison Weir's words 'the French had become a laughing stock in the eyes of the Muslim world and their reputation lay in the dust'.

The Saracens hand over the keys of Acre to King Phillip II of France and to King Richard the Lionheart.

King Phillip II of France picks a quarrel with King Richard the Lionheart at Messine. Permission to print both images given by Frederique Azmag.

The Third Crusade (1189-92) was aimed at the recapture of Jerusalem which had fallen to Saladin in 1187 after the overwhelming Saracen victory at the battle of Hattin. This Crusade was financed significantly in 1188 by King Henry II when he introduced the 'Saladin Tithe' payable in England, and also in France, by those who had not 'taken the Cross'. It was led by King Richard The Lionheart, who had just ascended the throne on the death of his father, and by King Philip II of France. It was a limited success. Richard captured Cyprus (it was lost to the Ottoman Empire in 1571) and in Palestine he had a brilliant victory at Arsuf against a mobile Muslim army attacking his baggage train. Another Crusaders' victory at Acre on the coast resulted in the shameful massacre of 2,700 Muslim prisoners. Moreover the Crusaders failed to capture Jerusalem. The Crusade ended with a negotiated Treaty between King Richard and Saladin, which gave minor concessions to the Latin Christians, access by unarmed Christians to the Holy Places in Jerusalem and safe passage home for the Crusaders (though Richard's return was somewhat delayed on his way back).

It is of interest to note that Hubert Walter, Bishop of Sarum 1189-93, was chief-of-staff to King Richard on this Crusade; and, after the signing of the peace treaty, took an unarmed party to visit the Holy Places in Jerusalem. He was received with honour by Saladin who offered him the choice of a parting present. Hubert asked that the two Latin (local) Christian priests should be allowed to serve at the Holy Sepulchre (the tomb in which Christ was laid), and at Bethlehem and Nazareth. Saladin readily agreed and the priests performed their rites unmolested. On his return to England Hubert Walter became Archbishop of Canterbury (1193-1205). Saladin died less than six months later on 4 March 1193.

The Fourth Crusade (c. 1202-04) was backed strenuously by Pope Innocent III and was led by Tibald, Count of Champagne and King of Navarre; and by Boniface, Marquis of Montferat and King of Thessalonika; and was accompanied by Enrico Dandolo, the Doge of Venice. Much to the angry surprise of the Pope and all the Christian Rulers in Europe the Crusader Army suddenly diverted north eastwards and savagely attacked their unfortunate allies in the ancient Byzantine city of Constantinople, magnificent centre of Eastern Christianity. They caused widespread destruction, killed many civilians, looted many churches and stole valuable religious relics and historic treasures some of which, today, may be discovered in Venice and many churches and museums around the world.

The result was irreparable damage to the Eastern Church and its ability to defend compatriots in the Latin principalities from increasingly well-organised attacks by the Saracens. Following the Fourth Crusade it was inevitable that the Church of Rome and the great Eastern Church should drift further apart. No amount of political and diplomatic activity by the leaders of the Western Christians could assuage the hatred felt by the Eastern Christians. As Sir Stephen Runciman says 'The schism between the two Christian movements was complete, irremediable and final. Fear of Western nations also raised a new fanaticism among some Muslims' (which, dare it be said, seems to have revived today).

It may be of interest to note that the Venetians were said to have had a total belief in the unicorn. The horns of two of these mythical beasts were kept in St Mark's Cathedral. A small quantity of horn was scraped off daily and fed to the ruling Doge to give him virility, health and longevity. The horns' elixir seems to have worked in the case of the partially blind Doge Enrico Dandolo who, in 1204 aged ninety six, was claimed to have been the first Western Christian over the walls at the siege of Constantinople. The horn-scraping was discontinued after this apparent success, the horns having been nearly eaten away by Dandolo (and his enthusiastic predecessors).

The Fifth Crusade (1218-21). The Fourth Lateran Council of 1215, presided over by Pope Innocent III, authorised individual clerical taxation to finance the Fifth Crusade led by Cardinal Pelagius of St Lucia and was aimed at the capture of Cairo, the subjugation of Egypt and then on to the capture of Jerusalem. But, after some success, there was a long delay and eventually the Crusaders were defeated by the Muslim Sultan al-Kamil at the first battle of Damietta. Pelagius sued for peace (no subsequent lessons were learned and, as will be seen later, history repeated itself in King Louis IX's First Crusade 1248-54 also known as the Seventh Crusade).

The Sixth Crusade (1228-29) was authorised by the elderly Pope Honorius III who died in 1227. It was led by Emperor Frederick II of Hohenstaufen (King of Germany) famous for his short-sighted green eyes, red hair and great intellect (he spoke six languages including Greek and Arabic). However he proved to be 'cruel, selfish and sly; an unreliable friend and an unforgiving enemy'. He was excommunicated by Pope Gregorious IX, Honorious's successor. Nevertheless he persuaded the Muslims to abandon Jerusalem in a Treaty witnessed by Peter des Roches the Bishop of Winchester and William the Bishop of Exeter, who were travelling with the English Crusader contingent. The city was lost once more to the Muslims in 1244 and they remained in control until 1917 with the start of the British Mandate.

The Costs of Crusading

Following promulgation by the Pope, command and control of a major international Crusade in the 12th and 13th centuries was an expensive business for European and Middle East royalty and potentates; the whole Christian Church; Crusader nobles, knights and their retainers, sergeants and ordinary soldiers and their families and friends at home. Muslim kingdoms, Emirates, provinces and city states were equally involved. Pope, King, Sultan and Emir did not hesitate to raise very heavy taxes to pay their fighting men and their administrative tails. Other major expenses for the European Crusaders included embarkation facilities; the hiring of shipping; supplies of food and fodder; arms and ammunition; siege machines (such as mangonels or missile throwers) and the construction of defensive fortifications and towers in foreign lands. Homelands had to be stabilised and left in charge of loyal regents. The lives of everyone – Christian and Muslim – were severely affected for centuries.

However the burden was not just financial. The loneliness of a Crusader's wife is graphically illustrated by this sad, and somewhat exotic, *little 'cri d'amour'*. *'It seems to me that I can feel (him) beneath my mantle of fur, and I regret very much that I was not there to see him on the road. He sent me his shirt which he had worn, so that I might hold it in my arms. At night, when love for him torments me, I place it beside me in bed and hold it through the night against my bare flesh to assuage my pain'* – taken from the Oxford Illustrated History of the Crusades edited by Jonathan Riley-Smith.

A great many Crusading husbands and fathers and brothers and, indeed, their Saracen opponents – the flower of several generations - never returned home, having died in battle or of wounds, or had perished from widespread diseases such as dysentery, plague and scurvy.

Some Muslim Reactions to the Western Christian Crusades. Jihad, the Holy War. Saladin's Arrival and Departure.

> *'Fight the unbelievers totally even as they fight you totally; and know that God is with the God-fearing'.*
>
> THE QU'RAN IX 36

Muslim Reactions to the Arrival of the First Crusade (1096-99)

The political situation among Muslim countries of the Middle East, before the start of the First Crusade, was affected by the growing disintegration of the northern Seljuk Empire of Rum and the weakness of the Fatimid Empire recently ensconced in Jerusalem. After the death of the Seljuk Sultan Malik Shah, in 1092, warring factions fought for supremacy. The historian, Robert Irwin, tells us how the Sunnis were the strongest group in this area and took their name from the Sunna who believed in the words and deeds of the Prophet Mohammed and his Companions, a body of orally transmitted tradition which helped shape both Islamic law (the Sharia) and the conduct of individual Muslims. The Sunnis recognised the supreme authority of the Caliphs. In this they differed from the Shi'i Muslims who believed that religion and political authority could only be held by 'Ali, the Prophet's son-in-law and, after that, by the Imams who were his descendants and spiritual successors. There were, much later, further developments and the Sunnis became very closely connected with the religious professors of Alhazar University in Egypt. Greater Syria (Syria, Lebanon and Palestine) became a moving battlefield after the collapse of the Seljuk

Empire. Turkomans and other groups invaded from the north, the Assassins ventured in from the south. The city of Damascus was at war with the city of Aleppo.

Jerusalem was not only sacred to the Christian pilgrims from the west; but it was also an Islamic Holy City too, and had a population of 20,000 Muslims. It was visited by Muslim pilgrims who found it too risky to visit Mecca or Medina. A pilgrimage to the important Muslim shrine of the Dome of the Rock, in the Temple Mount area of Jerusalem, had been the aim of devout Muslims from 692 AD.

When the first Christian Crusaders reached Greater Syria and the coastal ports of Eastern Mediterranean in 1096, local Muslim garrisons were reinforced by armies from Aleppo, Damascus and Mosul. But despite superior numbers these armies were disorganised and no match for the Crusaders who captured Antioch and Jerusalem and established Latin Christian settlements along the coast. The Muslim leaders and the Egyptian Vizier were not only taken by surprise; but were outraged at the atrocities committed by the Crusaders and were very angry at the loss of Jerusalem. However Islam remained largely disunited and war on their frontiers continued unabated.

Jihad (Holy War)

It was then that the theory of jihad (ie. 'Personal Struggle' or Holy War), originally outlined in the Qu'ran, became the order of the day and a rallying instruction for militant Islam. Jihad was not just a defensive war; but more a general obligation and a personal duty until the world could be brought firmly under the influence of Islam. Meanwhile the Sunnis replaced the Shi'ites in much of the Near East, the Assassins were driven back home and later defeated by their neighbours. Islam became more united along the coastal ports as their resistance to succeeding Crusades became better organised. The early Muslim refugees from Jerusalem, and the coastal areas settled in Aleppo and Damascus, turned to Jihad in the hope of returning to their homeland. All they needed was a leader.

Saladin's Arrival on the Scene

Eventually an army was sent by Nur-al-Din, Sultan of Damascus, to Egypt to counter the threat of Crusader ambitions. One of the generals was Saladin (Salah-al-Din loosely translated as Honour of the Faith) who was an Ayyub Kurd from the north. He took over the country when he was appointed Vizier in 1169 and proved to be an excellent diplomat winning the support of many local militant Muslim militias, soon becoming Sultan of Egypt and Syria.

On Sultan Nur's death in 1174 Saladin's army occupied Damascus; but it was not until 1183 that Saladin's military aims ceased to be the aggrandisement of his own family and friends and became a jihad against the Christian Crusaders and their Latin settlements.

Saladin's well-trained army comprised Kurds, Seljuks, other clans from the north, battalions of Mameluks (tough experienced slave soldiers) and even Western European mercenaries. An interesting and most effective, military tactic, introduced by Saladin on a large scale, was the use of Mameluk, Bedouin and Turkoman horsemen who fought in light cavalry formations. Robert Irwin notes that Saladin's elite troops were issued with the composite recurved bow made of layers of horn and sinews about a metre in length when unstrung. Unlike the Crusaders' bows they were offensive cavalry weapons and had more penetration power, and a longer range, than the French and English bows. The Mameluk horsemen were taught not only bare-back riding; but also how to fire their arrows backwards from the saddle. The rest of Saladin's army used simpler bows of which the arrows had considerably less force and little penetration. Muslim troops in close combat on the ground used light lances, javelins or swords and were protected by leather 'armour'. The Emirs (the officer class) and the Mameluk officers used lamillar (thin plates of metal), or chain mail, and were as heavily protected as their knightly Crusader opponents.

Saladin occupied Aleppo in 1183 and received the Overlordship of Mosul in 1186. In 1187 he crossed the river Jordan with an army of 20,000 of whom 12,000 were regular and experienced cavalry. Some of the rank and file included civilian jihadists whose duty it was to set alight the grass in advance of the Crusader armies. Saladin took on the army of Guy, King of Jerusalem, and defeated it sensationally at the Battle of Hattin in 1187. Most of the distinguished Christians taken in this battle were eventually ransomed but, says Robert Irwin, the Sufic ministers in Saladin's army were granted the privilege of beheading the Templar and Hospitaller prisoners. Saladin exploited his victory by occupying a series of weakly defended ports along the coast and then received the surrender of Jerusalem. This provoked the arrival of the Christian armies of the Third Crusade. Saladin conducted a war of attrition which compelled the latest Crusaders to sign a treaty allowing them to return home in safety and the Muslims to continue occupying Jerusalem. Saladin died of fever shortly after – a Muslim hero, worn out by implementation of his own jihad.

Chapter Seven

William Longespée II, Earl William's Eldest Son (1209-50). He is Knighted and Takes the Cross. The Seventh Crusade, Second Battle of Damietta and Sir William's Arrival in Egypt. Troubles with the French. The Fighting at Mansourah. Sir William Dies a Heroic Death. The French are Defeated and their King and Nobles are Captured, Bound in Chains, Ransomed and Released. France is Impoverished for a Generation. A Distinguished Historian Sums Up. Some More Descendents of Earl William and the Countess Ela. The DNA Factor! Salisbury Cathedral's Unknown Warrior.

'I shall not serve such a poor King'

Sir William Longespée II's outspoken criticism of King Louis IX and the French army in the early stages of the Seventh Crusade in the Middle East.

William is Knighted and Takes the Cross

Earl William and Countess Ela had four sons and four daughters. William the eldest, was born in 1209 and was only seventeen when his father died. While probably a minor William Longespée II became betrothed to Idonea, daughter and heiress of Richard de Camville and his wife Eustacia, daughter of Gilbert Basset and they were married sometime between 1226 and 1230. In 1230 he received his inheritance from his father and took part in Henry III's unfortunate expedition to Brittany in the same year. In 1233 King Henry III knighted him at Gloucester. In 1236 Sir William and his cousin, Richard Earl of Cornwall, together took the Cross at Worcester and in June 1240 they embarked on a minor Crusade to the Holy Land based on the city of Acre; but there was little military action and they returned to England in March 1242.

After his return from Acre he joined his cousin King Henry III in Gascony, when in July 1242, he distinguished himself at the battle of Saintes (the town of Saintes, today, is twinned with the city of Salisbury). He also took part in the raid on Pericord in late 1242 and in the siege of Garro in 1243. On returning to England he joined the royal expedition into Wales (1245) in response to the Welsh uprising of 1244-45 under Llywelyn ap Gruffidd. Meanwhile he pestered King Henry to give him the concomital (co-existent) title of Earl – but legal judgement was given against him (probably because his mother, the Countess Ela, had already inherited the title from her father). So he had to be content with his father's inheritance and many other lesser holdings i.e. he had plenty of land; but was short of a title, did not own a castle and had insufficient cash to fund his participation in a major Crusade.

During the Middle East Crusades of this period, taking the Cross meant a personal and public vow to recover the Holy Land from the Saracens (a name given to any member of the nomadic peoples of the Syrian and Arabic deserts which harassed the borders of the Roman Empire – later identified as an Arab, a Turk or a Muslim, specially during the time of the Crusades). The Crusaders' military aims were to protect pilgrims travelling along the road from the coast to Jerusalem and to safeguard the Holy Places from marauding bands of Saracens. Those taking part believed in the subsequent remission of sins and a guaranteed place in Heaven. It also involved safeguards for families left behind, the raising of substantial sums of money, often by dubious means, and the wearing of a coloured Cross on outer clothing.

Like his father, Sir William was a religious man. He patronised the Franciscans of Sarum and Oxford and the Dominicans of Wilton. He gave substantial donations to Lacock Abbey,

Bradenstoke Priory and various other religious institutions founded by his family. Over the years he went on pilgrimages to shrines in Europe including one to Santiago de Compostella. He took the Cross again in May 1247.

So, it was not easy for Sir William Longespée, in 1247, to carry out his responsibilities to the Cross for the second time. He had not been allowed to inherit an earldom, with all its attendant perquisites; moreover, he was still short of estates, employees of military age and money. The chronicler Mathew Paris explains his delicate situation thus *'William, in hopes of reaping where he had not sowed, quietly collected money from people who had already taken the Cross. He also went to the Papal curia in Lyons and persuaded the Pope 'My Lord, as you see, I have already taken the sign of the Cross, and I am ready to fight for God by journeying with the King of the French. I have a great and famous name, William Longespée, but little property or money. So I am forced to apply to your paternal generosity and ask for your help in my need. I venture to request that I, in need and having taken the Cross, be granted your favour'. The Lord Pope, considering the eloquence of the speaker, the cogency of his reasoning and the handsomeness of his person, was favourably disposed towards him and granted him part of what he asked, namely a thong from another man's skin'* (the meaning of the thong in the last part of Parish's quote is curious but obscure).

The ODNB notes that Sir William Longespée had great difficulty in persuading the Pope of his financial problems and the need for a substantial assignment of Papal cash. Additional money was raised by him from the lease of four of his manors and the grant of a charter to the burgesses of Poole. Further grants came from his royal patron and other relatives. Before his departure on the Crusade he settled property disputes to ensure the security of his own interests and those of his family. He drew up his will (duly confirmed by the King), the securing of royal judicial protection in his absence, the appointment of executors and attorneys and the conclusion of a number of quitclaims and final concords. In 1249 he secured from his mother, the Abbess of Lacock, that he would receive all spiritual benefits and prayers of her House in perpetuity. It was also probable that he requested his body be buried in Lacock Abbey. He seems to have left England in late June, or early July 1249 in command of around two hundred English knights and their retinues. He joined King Louis IX of France's army at Damietta in Egypt during late 1249 before the Crusaders' advance up the Nile.

The Start of the Seventh Crusade and The Battle of Damietta 1249

Having rebuilt and fortified the port of Aigues Mortes, south of the Camargue in France, Louis IX, his wife Margaret the Queen, together with the advance guard of the French armies and 'mountains of wine', embarked on 28 August 1248 for Limassol in Cyprus. They wintered there while the king's diplomacy failed to obtain military support from potential allies e.g. the Mongols who were busily extending their frontiers westward. Worse still his security was lax and Egyptian spies concluded that he was preparing to land in Egypt at either Alexandria or Damietta, rather than further north in Latin Palestine, as first thought. In March 1249 the French fleet re-assembled off Limassol and the army boarded the transports. Suddenly a great storm brewed up, leaving only a quarter of the fleet intact and the rest scattered over the eastern Mediterranean. On 20 May the king decided to re-embark and sailed towards the port of Damietta in Northern Egypt.

The landing was strongly opposed by superior Saracen forces. The Crusaders, led by the king himself, prevailed and the Saracens fled leaving an open city. The Crusaders marched in triumphantly and then waited for reinforcements from Cyprus, and for the flood waters of the Nile to recede, prior to advancing by road and river towards Cairo. The Great Mosque in Damietta became a Christian cathedral and a Bishop was installed.

The Muslim world was shocked. Their Sultan offered to exchange Damietta for Jerusalem; but King Louis stubbornly refused to treat with an 'infidel'. Many Muslim Emirs were executed by their countrymen for cowardice in action and more Muslim troops were rushed up to Mansourah (meaning 'victorious' in English). This town had been built by Sultan al-Kamil in 1221 on the site of his earlier triumph over Cardinal Pelagius, Pope Honorious III's appointed leader of the Fifth Crusade. A few days later the aged Sultan Ayub, the last great member of the widely respected and powerful Ayubite dynasty, died. His widowed Sultana, Shajar ad-Durr, and Fakhr ad-Din took over as Regents pending the arrival from Syria of Ayub's only son Turanshah.

The Saracens recovered quickly from their reverses and set about blocking King Louis' road to Cairo, cutting off his lines of supply by road and river around Damietta. King Louis, belatedly realising the dangers of isolation, overcame his former reluctance and offered to exchange the port of Damietta for the city of Jerusalem, still firmly in Saracen hands; but much too late and to no avail, for the Saracens believed that time was now on their side and they were in a very strong military position. Instead, they mounted a furious attack on the French around Mansourah.

Sir William Arrives in Egypt. His Early Military Successes.

Mathew Paris noted in his contemporary chronicle that when Sir William Longespée joined King Louis' army in Egypt in July 1249 he found the French not only 'lay rotting and muddled by drink and incompetent leadership'; but also they took great delight in calling the English soldiers 'long-tailed cowards' (an expression which depicted the English as having tails fixed to them as a punishment for the murder of Archbishop Thomas Becket in 1170). Nevertheless Sir William Longespée and the English contingent achieved notable early successes, gaining a reputation for bravery in battle and the acquisition of a great deal of booty from plundering Saracen baggage trains, which made the French soldiers thoroughly envious and very angry. An example of French envy of Sir William Longespée, as quoted by Paris, concerns his capture of a certain strongly fortified tower, not far from Alexandria, full of noble Saracen ladies. Paris does not enlarge on the fate of these ladies but, perhaps, latent chivalry and irresistible greed combined to intervene; and they may well have been ransomed for large sums of money by their male relatives.

Personal Relations Between the English and the French Soldiers

Relations between the English and French became so bad that Sir William Longespée requested the French king to control his men. However the French king who was at loggerheads with his brother, Robert the Count of Artois, a senior commander of the French army, was quite unable to do so. Thereupon William declared 'I shall not serve such a poor king' and took his contingent to Acre, where he joined the Hospitallers and the Templars. Later King Louis provided Sir William with 'every satisfaction for the insults he had received'. William was mollified and rejoined the French army in Egypt.

William's Return to French Army Headquarters.
First Battle of Mansourah.

On his return to French headquarters he found the French were preparing a major assault on the Egyptian army which was encamped across the River Nile. He discovered that the impetuous Count Robert of Artois was about to lead an advance party across the river; so he and his men, together with the Master of the Templars, joined them – not realising that Robert had deliberately omitted to obtain King Louis' agreement to advance, being intent solely on obtaining glory for himself. Count Robert's troops crossed the river and launched an attack on the fortified Saracen town of Mansourah. Having killed everyone they could find they demolished the fortifications and forced their way into the centre; but there they were ambushed by a hail of well-aimed stones and had to withdraw. Not to be outdone Count Robert of Artois declared his intention to mount an immediate counter-attack on the Saracens. But William de Saunac, Master of the Templars and widely experienced in military matters, said 'Our troops are tired, hungry and thirsty. We also need to revive our wounded comrades and our exhausted horses. We should await the arrival of the king and his army and then make an all-out attack on the demoralised Saracens, (still mourning the death of their Sultan). We need to be reunited and speak with one voice'.

More Trouble With The French

The Count of Artois became excited at this and, flushed with anger and pride, exclaimed 'See the time-honoured treachery of the Temple ! The ancient sedition of the Hospitallers ! …..the whole country of the East would have been conquered long ago had it not been for the Templars and the Hospitallers who have hindered us, the laymen, with their deceit. These Templars and Hospitallers and their associates, fattened by ample revenues, are afraid that, if the country is subject to Christian laws, their supremacy will come to an end'. To which the Master of the Templars said to his standard-bearer in a loud voice 'Unfurl and raise our banner. We shall advance to battle and experience together, today, the uncertain fortunes of war and the chance of death. We would have been insuperable had we remained inseparable; but, unfortunately, we are divided, like sand without water, so that we are unfit for spiritual edifice and, lacking the cement of mutual affection, we shall forthwith become like ruined walls'.

Sir William Longespée, greatly fearing the schism engendering in the army, said 'The Master of the Temple is a sincere and noble man and has been resident in the East for a long time ….. and knows the strength and craftiness of the Saracens. No wonder that we, newcomers, young men and foreigners are ignorant of the ways of the East. As far distant as the East is from the West, so far different are Westerners from the Orientals'. But Robert shouted, as the French do, and swearing indecently, gave tongue to the following invective in the hearing of many 'How cowardly these timid people with tails are ! How blessed, how clean this army would be, if purged of tails and tailed people !'. The shamed William, provoked and upset by these insulting words, replied 'Count Robert, I shall most certainly proceed undismayed by any peril of impending death. We shall be today, I fancy, where you will not dare to touch my horse's tail'.

Further Fighting at Mansourah.
Heroic Death of Sir William Longespée.

And so the Battle of Mansourah took place on 6 February 1250. The tired French and English troops, cut off from the main French army, were no match for the fresh Saracen reinforcements who were united as never before under their newly appointed Sultan, Turanshar. Eventually the Count of Artois called on William to escape. Came the reply "God forbid that my father's son should fly for any Saracen – I would rather die happily than live unhappily". William and his standard-bearer, Robert de Vere, together with all but a few Englishmen, were slain. The Count was ignominiously drowned in a river whilst fleeing from the battle.

The Saracens, their Sultan and the Mameluk officers (the Mameluks were an army corps of Turkish and Circassian slaves) declared Sir William Longespée to have been the bravest soldier of all time. A poet of the day described William's death in these words *'First, his left foot was cut off, causing him to dismount from his horse and support himself with the help of a French knight. As he continued to fight on foot, his right arm was severed. Transferring his sword to his left hand, he exchanged blows with a Saracen and killed him. Then William fell to the ground, where he was cut to pieces by a swarm of foes'*. The Saracens gave him an honourable burial and, later, reproached the Christians for leaving his tomb uncared for. They obtained leave to remove his bones and interred him reverently in the Church of The Holy Cross at Acre. Thus, his wish to be buried in Lacock Abbey was unfulfilled.

Countess Ela, now Holy Abbess of Lacock, has a Dream

Mathew Paris closes his dramatic version of Sir William Longespée's death with this account by the Holy Abbess of a vision seen by her *"whilst I was day-dreaming in my stall at Lacock during the night preceding the battle, I saw a Knight, completely equipped in armour, received into the heavens, which were open to greet him. I recognised the Knight's shield and enquired with astonishment the identity of the Knight, who had been received in such glory by the angels. The reply came in a clear and distinct voice 'It is your son, William'. I took note of the date and time'*. The awful news from Egypt reached me later".

Paris goes on to relate 'Following confirmation of the death in Egypt of her eldest son, she remembered the glorious vision of him at the very moment of his death. She clasped her hands and knelt down exclaiming 'My Lord Jesus Christ, I give Thee thanks that you have wished such a son to be procreated from my body, unworthy sinner that I am, whom you have deigned to adorn with the crown of such manifest martyrdom. I certainly hope that, with his help, I shall speedily be promoted to the heights of the heavenly kingdom'. Those present praised her more than womanly steadfastness, wondering at her motherly and maternal piety, which did not express itself in words of querulous lament; but rather excelled cheerfully in spiritual joy'. Ela herself died eleven and a half years later.

The Final Battle of Mansourah.
The French and their Allies are Defeated.

When the main French army, once again led personally by their king, joined the battle they achieved an early victory and recovered most of the town of Mansourah. But, eventually, strong Saracen reinforcements, under Sultan Turanshah, resumed the attack and overwhelmed the Crusaders, taking many prisoners.

The French Surrender. The King is Imprisoned.
The Queen Intervenes.

The resourceful and intrepid Queen Margaret, while acting as 'quartermaster' for the garrison in Damietta, discovered she was in the last stages of pregnancy and gave birth to a son under the supervision of an octogenarian knight, acting as midwife. Three days later, the French army surrendered to the Saracens. King Louis was captured soon after, put in chains and imprisoned. Having named her newly-born son Jean Tristan (child of sorrow),

Queen Margaret immediately set about negotiating the ransoms and release of her husband and his two surviving brothers.

The Final Act

Although negotiations on the ransoms of the surviving nobles and knights also began in earnest, a great many rank and file Crusaders and civilians were caught and beheaded by the Saracens ('three hundred a day', says historian Sir Stephen Runciman). Their soldiers, including the pagan Mameluk slaves, frequently ignored the terms of the surrender and created havoc among the unfortunate population of Damietta. Eventually the king, the queen and part of the French army were permitted to return to Acre and, having reorganised themselves, took part in the second phase of their Crusade. However the majority of the survivors, who had been ransomed and released, took ship for France. As a result of these ransoms, and the accumulated costs of the Crusade, France was impoverished for a generation.

A short while later the Mameluk soldiers mutinied and murdered Sultan Turanshah and appointed their commanding officer, Izz ad-Din Aibek, as Regent. He promptly persuaded the Dowager Sultana, Shajar, to marry him thus acquiring a modicum of legitimacy.

The chroniclers tell us 'The entire Christian army, alas! comprising the nobility of France, the Knights of the Temple and the Hospital; the Teutonic Knights of St Mary; and the Knights of St Lazarus and Sir William Longespée were slaughtered or captured. The Pope and the entire Roman curia ..... daily lost favour with both clergy and people ..... the whole of Christianity was troubled ..... those who died were proclaimed martyrs ..... their names to be inscribed indelibly in the Book of Life'.

The full story of the defeat of King Louis IX's Crusading army is described in much gory detail by Jean de Joinville in his Chronicles of King Louis IX's First Crusade. He fought beside his king throughout this Crusade and was captured, imprisoned and later released by the Saracens. He defends, with spirit, the Canonisation of King Louis and pays many personal tributes to his monarch's exceptional leadership qualities, his outstanding bravery in battle, his unfailing love of God and his complete disregard of worldly vanities. He was also a witness at the investigation leading to the Canonisation of King Louis IX in 1298.

Having arrived in Acre with a small remnant of his army, King Louis entered into a long series of diplomatic negotiations with surrounding Muslim potentates; the Mameluks, now ensconced in Egypt and the Mongols to the East. He was more successful at these than he had been as a military commander. However the situation had changed as a result of his defeat in Egypt. The king's mother, the Queen Regent of France, had died in November 1252 and public support within France for another Crusade was out of the question. Moreover King Henry III of England, despite having taken the Cross, also declined to send reinforcements. Sir Stephen Runciman concludes 'Although his sojourn at Acre did much to repair the damage of the Egyptian disaster, the loss of manpower could never be recovered. Louis had the noblest character of all the latest Crusaders. The king and his entourage left Acre for France in 1254. He later went to Tunis on another disastrous Crusade in 1264, and died there a broken man in August 1267 – his last words were 'Jerusalem, Jerusalem'.

Sir Stephen Runciman, in his final summing up of the Middle East Crusades, concludes 'There was so much courage and so little honour; so much devotion and so little understanding. High ideals were besmirched by cruelty and greed; enterprise and endurance by a blind narrow-righteousness; and the Holy War itself was nothing more than a long act of intolerance in the name of God. The whole Crusading movement was a complete fiasco'.

Author's Comment: It is difficult to accept all Sir Stephen Runciman's final conclusions above. In the early days (late 11th century) it would have been impossible for the widely respected Pope Urban II to ignore the worsening military situation in the Holy Land and the sufferings of the Christian, Jewish and Muslim communities in Jerusalem; nor would a French King, of the character and status of Philip II Auguste of France or, indeed, the many chivalrous knights in the countries of Western Europe turn a blind eye to the fate of Jerusalem. It is also relevant to note that the Crusaders brought back to Europe such benefits as Arab learning, numbers, music and musical instruments; also a variety of new food and Arab history which contributed much to the 12th century Renaissance and a completely fresh understanding of the Middle East and its inhabitants.

Some More Longespée Descendants and the DNA Factor!

Sir William Longespée II's Family

As already stated, he married Idonea. Their eldest son William Longespée III died in 1256. This third William Longespée married Maud, daughter and heir of William de Clifford of Clifford Castle in Hereford. Their little daughter, Margaret, the great grand-daughter to Ela, Countess of Salisbury, became de jure the second Countess of Salisbury on the death of her father, when she was aged two. Margaret married Henry de Laci Earl of Lincoln; but she did not use her title. Their daughter, Alice de Laci, suo jure was Countess of Lincoln and Salisbury. She married three times. On her death the title passed to a descendant of Ela, the third daughter of William Longespée II and Idonea de Camville by her marriage to James de Audley, Justiciar of Ireland.

Their Second Son Richard (styled as a Knight in 1242)

Sir Richard Longespée appears to have taken Holy Orders late in life and became a Canon of Salisbury Cathedral. He was buried at Lacock Abbey.

Their Third Son Stephen

Stephen Longespée became a competent soldier and administrator. He was appointed Seneschal of Gascony in 1254. In 1258 the control of Sherborne Castle was given to him by Henry III and he also became Constable of Corfe Castle. The following year he was appointed Lord Justice of Ireland and died in that office during 1260. He married Emeline de Redelesford, Countess of Ulster and widow of Hugh de Laci, Earl of Ulster. His body was buried in Lacock Abbey, and his heart at Bradenstoke Priory (the aforementioned family residence).

Their Fourth Son Nicholas

Nicholas Longespée may have taken Holy Orders late in life and became a Canon of Salisbury Cathedral and was its Treasurer by 1271. He became Rector of Lacock Abbey in 1290 until his appointment to Salisbury as Bishop, in 1291. He may have added the decorated wooden tomb chest to his father's memorial in order to make it even grander. He died in 1297. His heart was buried at Lacock, his viscera (internal organs) at Ramsbury and his body at the entrance of the Trinity Chapel in Salisbury Cathedral. His chalice, paten and Episcopal ring are usually displayed in the Cathedral's Chapter House. Sadly, the site of his burial was destroyed by James Wyatt c. 1790.

Earl William's and Countess Ela's Four Daughters

The first, Isobella, married William de Vesci, a baron of Northumberland, and died without issue in 1248. The second, Petronella, died young and unmarried and was buried at Bradenstoke Priory. The third, Ela, married, firstly, the Earl of Warwick, and, secondly, Philip Basset, Justiciar of England, she died without issue and was buried at Osney in Oxfordshire. The fourth daughter, Ida, married firstly Walter Fitz-Richard by whom she had one son and three daughters and, secondly, she married William Beauchamp of Bedford, by whom she had a further three sons (all of whom died without issue) and three daughters.

Subsequent Creations of the Salisbury Earldom

There followed various new creations, forfeitures and restorations of the Earldom of Salisbury involving the Laci, Montacute, Audley, Montague, Nevill and Plantagenet families. The present Earldom, according to Debrett, goes back to a fresh creation in 1605 when Lord High Treasurer Burleigh's elder son, Thomas Cecil, was created Earl of Exeter; and his younger son, Robert Cecil was, on the same day, created Earl of Salisbury.

Connections with the House of Windsor

Genealogical research by the historian Linda K Jack states that, in the 14th century, one of William Longespée's third son Stephen's descendants was Thomas Holland, the second Earl of Kent, who produced a large family from whom two daughters, Eleanor and Margaret would make historic marriages. Eleanor married Roger Mortimer, fourth Earl of March; and Margaret married John Beaufort, first Earl of Somerset. The descendants of these two earls were King Richard III and Henry Tudor. They clashed during the War of the Roses on 22nd August 1485 at the Battle of Bosworth Field. Richard III was killed and that was the end of the Plantagenet dynasty. Henry Tudor, sporting the red rose, prevailed. He married Elizabeth of York of the white rose faction and became Henry VII, thus combining the two roses into the Tudor rose and founding the Tudor dynasty. Queen Elizabeth II is the thirteenth great grand-daughter of King Henry VII and, so it appears, is also a direct descendant of William Longespée, Earl of Salisbury.

Other descendants of William Longespée are said by Linda Jack to have emigrated to North America and number among their descendants the following six American Presidents: George Washington, Thomas Jefferson, James Madison, Theodore Roosevelt Jnr, George Bush Snr and George W Bush Jnr. (I note in passing that an American couple touring Salisbury Cathedral, with me as their guide, showed me lengthy documents outlining their claim that she was directly descended from Earl William Longespée too).

The DNA Factor!

If one examines the effects of DNA on some 30 subsequent generations of the original Earl William Longespée family, then a very large number of Longespée's descendants might be able to trace their family back to William 3rd Earl of Salisbury and well beyond that too.

Some Observations on Salisbury Cathedral's Unknown Medieval Warrior. Comments on the Crossing of Legs.

The effigy of a knight, suitably accoutred with helmet, plain shield and full body armour, his body stiff and unrelaxed and his legs devoutly crossed may be seen at the west end of Salisbury cathedral's north aisle. Some have said that this effigy is of William Longespée II, the eldest son of the Third Earl of Salisbury. However the Senior Curator of the Royal Armouries at Leeds, together with colleagues and historians, conclude that, while one can never be absolutely certain on such matters, it is extremely unlikely that it commemorates Sir William, who died abroad in 1250. His armour almost certainly dates to well within the 14th century. An earlier date cannot be taken seriously since it is unsupported by any known evidence; cathedral archives not having revealed (so far) any reliable information on the identification of the effigy. So this knightly cenotaph may be described as that of an unknown warrior of the 14th century.

Professor Brian Kemp, of Reading University, too, says that this cenotaph is certainly not of Sir William Longespée, eldest son of the third Earl of Salisbury. Nevertheless he observes, 'it is of great interest. The warrior depicted is clearly not at rest; he is shown in the act of drawing his sword and is wearing boiled leather protection for his elbows and knees. Moreover he has a rowel at the end of the spur on his right ankle; this feature would not have appeared when his death was remembered. The crossed legs do not necessarily signify death abroad on a Crusade. It almost certainly depicts a man on foot showing deference to another person (perhaps, to his Maker or to his monarch, or both). However some Crusader effigies have their thighs crossed which would make deference from an upright position somewhat difficult to perform with dignity. The crossed legs, and probably the placement of animals which support the feet, were examples of the changing fashion in English monumental design in the period 1275-1350. They were an English feature and do not appear in French churches although, of course, France was very much the leading Crusading nation'.

Comment on the configuration of the legs, and its likely relevance to service in the Crusades, became popular in the Victorian romantic Gothic-revival period (when, perhaps, this association with Sir William Longespée may have developed) and then taken up with enthusiasm by poets and painters of the day, such as found in one of William Wordsworth's Ecclesiastical Sonnets, which reads in part

> *'Furl we the sails, and pass with tardy oars*
> *Through these bright regions, casting many a glance*
> *Upon the dream-like issues – the romance*
> *Of many coloured life that Fortune pours*
> *Round the Crusaders, till on distant shores*
> *Their labours end; or they return to lie,*
> *The vow performed, in cross legged effigy,*
> *Devoutly stretched upon their chancel floors'.*

The Rev Simon Lloyd historian notes 'the fine knightly effigy in the nave of Salisbury Cathedral is said, traditionally, to be of (William Longespée II) and produced on his mother's order, but the grounds for this are no more than romantic'.

Chapter Eight

Pope Honorius III's Bull of 1218. Preparatory Building Work Begins. The Original Plan. William de Waude Praises Bishop Richard Poore, the Driving Force Behind Salisbury Cathedral's 13th Century Transfer in Unbroken Succession from Old to New Sarum. Richard Poore's Early Life. The Use of Sarum. His Interest in the Education of Children. His Palace. His Omnicompetent Designer Elias de Durham. The Royal Palace at Clarendon. Bishop Poore's Translation to Durham Cathedral 1228. His Death in 1237.

'You are a Chosen Generation … a Particular People … You should Shew Forth the Praises of Him who has Called You out of Darkness into His Marvellous Light'.

I ST PETER 2.9

Pope Honorius III Issues his Bull 1218

The elderly Bishop Herbert Poore, who might have supervised the move, ran out of money and energy. So the prospect of building a new cathedral began to fade. However, following the deaths of King John and Pope Innocent III, the defeat of Prince Louis of France and his ignominious return to his homeland produced an unexpected rapid change in fortunes. The new Pope, Honorious III issued his Bull in 1218 licensing a move of Sarum cathedral in 'unbroken succession' to the chosen site which eventually became 'Salisbury'.

Preparatory Work on the New Site Begins

The cathedral site soon became a huge storehouse of stones, wood, glass and lead. The builders set up their different workshops nearby i.e. the plumbers, carpenters, masons, painters, decorators etc. Inside the cathedral is an interesting well-designed model of the cathedral under construction at the halfway stage. In the chapter house today there is a renovated antique medieval table on which labourers would have been paid at the average rate of a penny farthing a day. Tatton-Brown notes 'work must have been pushed along at full speed. Five foot deep trenches would have been dug all round the site of the proposed cathedral. The basic design would have started from the square forming the main crossing and then along the nave to the west.

By 1226 all the outside walls would have been built up to a height of between seven and eight feet, high enough to take the consecration crosses and founding stones. The latter were not like the ordinary blocks used for the laying ceremonies on 28 April 1220. They were large rounded stones with the crosses carved on each and carrying a unique engraved brass plate. Priority had also been given to the completion of the three chapels at the east end'.

He continues, 'by the end of 1225, the east end and the three chapels originally dedicated to St Stephen, the Trinity and St Peter had been finished as had much of the rest of the eastern arm of the cathedral. The use of slender columns of Purbeck marble (actually, shelly limestone) indicate the splendour of this part of the cathedral.

Modern dendrochronology (the science of dating wood by examination of rings and original bark) showed that the roof, and the east end itself, dated precisely to the year 1222. Some of the wood used was Irish oak illustrating again the rush to complete the east end. Wood was sought from everywhere, it was only later that a sufficient bank of wood was obtained from the king's local forests. The foundation trenches dug before 1220 were not haphazard but very carefully constructed down to the layer of impacted gravel five feet below. The bases of the trenches were made smooth to take the layers of stone on top'.

Tatton-Brown concludes

'In these early days, there was no question of building just another cathedral. It was one and the same cathedral and the physical transfer of the cathedral to the new site was part of a continuing story. The two cathedrals never operated separately, it was a case of *the cathedral is dead, long live the cathedral*. There was no break and it was certainly Bishop Osmund who provided the inspiration, the link and the continuity. Although the builders of Salisbury cathedral had no access to modern civil engineering, at least they inherited a hundred years of massive cathedral building experience all over England. Unlike Winchester cathedral, much of which was built over a watery marsh, Salisbury's virgin ground was the best possible place to build. The bishops, canons and local lords were very rich indeed and they had access to a youthful co-operative king and a court much influenced by the church in a part of the country largely at peace with itself'.

The Original Plan

Sarah Brown, historian of Salisbury Cathedral and expert on medieval glass and decoration, says 'Salisbury Cathedral was planned and constructed in an almost unbroken single build and was provided with rich furnishings by a succession of generous bishops and by a Chapter with close links to the Court. And yet it is now exceptionally difficult to visualise the original context for these medieval furnishings and decorations ... the effects of late medieval reordering, the Reformation, iconoclasm and misguided restoration have all taken their toll ... the original décor of Salisbury Cathedral, a rich vision of the heavenly Jerusalem, is now lost to us'.

Sarah Brown observes that 'The cathedral's interior was originally covered in paint, and in some places with gilding. The rendering and painting of masonry was a common feature of most great churches and Salisbury was no exception. Red masonry lines, in imitation of ashlar, covered the vault webs and the walls, augmented by red, green and some black used to articulate the vault ribs and, in the eastern arm, the moulding of the triforium arcade and clerestory windows. The overall effect would have been suggested by the architecture itself, where light masonry contrasted with the darker Purbeck accents and echoed by the effect of the paint; and was far richer than that sought by the 18th century 'improvers' who covered the entire interior with a buff wash'.

and

'The richest painted decoration was reserved for the choir, presbytery and eastern transepts, with its rich figurative scheme on the vaults and sumptuous foliage decoration in the spandrels of the main arcade and on the eastern wall, marking out the choir as the heart of the cathedral's devotional life. Twenty four figure medallions, depicting Christ in Majesty, the Evangelist, Prophets, Patriarchs, Apostles, and the Sibylls, with the Annual Labours of the twelve months over the presbytery and an angelic host in each of the eastern transepts were displayed above the heads of the cathedral clergy'.

Sarah Brown continues further 'The 19th century repainting of the Trinity Chapel and retrochoir vaults, on the other hand, quite successfully suggests the nature of the 13th century scheme, restrained when compared with the choir. The imitation ashlaring is augmented with wedges of foliage ornament and mouldings are picked out in red, green and black. It was here, however, that stained glass was used to great effect. For much of the

Middle Ages the most substantial areas of bright colour in the Trinity Chapel would have been supplied by its windows, only eclipsed in the 15th century by the gold and jewel-encrusted shrine of St Osmund which later became its focus'. Careful examination of the inside of the cathedral's north wall, the choir and the eastern transepts will reveal faint outlines of the original 13th century painting.

Sarah Brown, again 'The Jesse Tree fragments now in the south aisle of the nave, would have fitted both physically and iconographically, into the east window of the Trinity Chapel which was, de facto, a Lady Chapel and the site of the daily Mass of the Virgin; although, by the end of the 18th century, the glass had been moved first into the north transept and then into the nave. A Jesse window, depicting in visual terms the ancestry of Christ, had become a standard subject in the great churches of the 12th and 13th centuries.

William de Waude Praises the Appointment of Bishop Richard Poore

William de Waude (sometimes referred to as de Wanda), Precentor then Dean of Old Sarum Cathedral (elected 1220), and contemporary chronicler, describes Bishop Richard Poore 'as a man of the greatest learning as well as of the purist morals ...the nation had found him a loyal and excellent champion against Louis, son of the King of France, and his frenchmen, who, at that time were come over to take possession of the kingdom. Richard's translation to Sarum on the death of Bishop Herbert Poore, his half-brother, was what everyone wished, what God provided, what the Pope (Honorius III) supported and what the universe required'.

Bishop Herbert Poore of Old Sarum Cathedral 1194 - 1217. Half brother to Bishop Richard Poore of Old and New Sarum 1217 - 1228.

Bishop Richard Poore's Family

Richard Poore's half-brother Herbert was born c. 1140 at about the time his father Richard of Ilchester, a Royal Judge, was created Bishop of Winchester (1140-80). His parents never married. He spent many years in the King's service before being appointed Bishop of Salisbury (1194-1217). Richard Poore was born c. 1160 to the same father, but a different mother who his father never married; she may have been associated with the Tarrant area of Dorset, near Blandford Forum. Richard himself was generally known as Richard Poore. There seemed to be no records to indicate whence the name Poore came. Richard later obtained a Papal dispensation for his illegitimacy, so removing any bar to a future bishopric.

His Education. Elected Dean of Sarum Cathedral. Exile in France.

Richard would have been educated locally, then at Sarum, presumably in the Cathedral Choir School founded by Bishop Osmund. He proceeded to the University of Paris c. 1180 where he would have come under the influence of Lotario de Conti de Signi, later to become Pope Innocent III. His English tutor in the University of Paris was Stephen Langton, an eminent biblical scholar from Lincolnshire (who first divided the Bible into chapters and later, on the Pope's insistence and against the wishes of King John, became Archbishop of Canterbury). Richard was said to have been 'an apt pupil' and later became 'a graduate and master' of the university.

Following Richard Poore's return to Salisbury he became actively involved with his half-brother Herbert and Bishop Hubert Walter in detailed planning for the new cathedral. He was elected Dean (1198-1215) and was unsuccessfully nominated for the Sees of Winchester in 1205 and Durham in 1213. Both half-brothers went into exile throughout Pope Innocent III's interdict over England (1208-1213/14). Richard returned to Paris University and taught theology and, according to Virginia Jansen, historian, acted as a 'Papal Judge and Delegate' on at least six occasions.

Nominated Bishop of Chichester. Attended 4th Lateran Council. Becomes Bishop of Sarum.

Richard was nominated Bishop of Chichester (1215-1217) and was a witness when King John reluctantly placed his double-sided seal on Magna Carta in 1215 at Runnymede. In the same year he spent a great deal of time in Rome during the 4th Lateran Council (dominated completely by his friend the ageing, but still powerful, Pope Innocent III). He stayed on in Rome attending numerous subsequent meetings, drafting Papal proclamations, converting policy decisions into practical requirements of the church, dealing with petitions and obtaining legal rulings. Herbert, old and feeble, did not attend the Council and died in January 1217. He was buried at Wilton and was succeeded as Bishop of Sarum by his half-brother Richard.

The European stage began to change dramatically. Not only had Richard's half-brother Bishop Herbert died; but also both King John and Pope Innocent III died in 1216. A new Pope, Honorius III, had just been elected to the Papal See; King John's son, a boy aged nine, King Henry III, was on the throne of England; the Royalists had defeated the rebel barons. Peace and reconciliation were the orders of the day: and Richard was free to become seriously involved in planning and executing his move of the cathedral from Old Sarum to New Sarum (Salisbury). He was assisted greatly in implementing these plans by the Cardinal Legate, Gualo Biechieri, who administered the Pope's affairs in England.

Bishop Richard Poore holding a model of his half completed Cathedral.

In 1219 he also approved the final plans for the city of Salisbury, some of which were already being implemented, which would provide accommodation for the workers building the new cathedral. These divided the city into chequers, irregular roads and a number of canals with separate areas for each trade and, of course, several inns. Richard became a royal justice in 1218 and 1219. In 1223 when Peter des Roches, the Bishop of Winchester, fell from power, Richard was one of a small group of famous men who helped Hubert de Burgh take over the Regency Government of England.

Richard also became a close friend and companion of Henry III throughout his minority and early adult years. He was required to be present whenever the king issued proclamations. He became a great traveller on the king's business and visited Westminster at least fifteen times and a great many other places in middle and southern England. He rode everywhere, it was said, 'stopping off and dismounting only to baptise children'. He continued to be closely involved with implementing the move to New Sarum.

The Use of Sarum

While Richard was Dean of Salisbury he introduced a set of practical rules and regulations for the cathedral and later on, as Bishop, he wrote the Sarum Use which soon became general practice throughout most of the country with little variation. The Rev Professor Canon J. Robert Wright, of the Anglican Society, has written

'The Sarum Use is the name applied to the particular rendering of divine worship in the English Church that was developed at Salisbury, in Wiltshire, from the early 13th century and then gradually spread to become at least by the 14th century, the finest local expression of the Western or Roman Rite in England up to the Reformation'. He continues 'The Sarum Use, then, was a rather exuberant, elaborate, beautiful, and especially well arranged adaptation of the Western or Roman Rite that was gradually adopted by most of the rest of England as well as much of Wales, Scotland, Ireland and even some places on the continent. Indeed, the first Sarum Missal to be printed was at Paris in 1487, then Basle 1489, Rouen 1492, Venice 1494, etc. and not at London until 1498'.

Canon Professor Wright also says
'Origins: The Norman Conquest (1066) ushered in not only a widespread enlargement and rebuilding of cathedrals and churches; but also continental influences tending towards the centralisation of both liturgy and monastic customs. Even earlier, this could be seen in the *Regularis Concordia of c. 970, and, after the Conquest, in the Monastic Constitutions of Archbishop Lanfranc (Archbishop of Canterbury 1070-89)*, who was born in Italy, and became a biblical scholar of international repute and was responsible for rebuilding Canterbury Cathedral, and authorising the building of Salisbury Cathedral). Parallel, and subsequent to these developments, there seems to have been a need felt for a certain clarity and fixity in liturgical matters at the secular (non-monastic) cathedrals'.

He continues
'There has been much discussion and debate over who was actually instrumental in the development of the Sarum Use. 19th century scholars generally attributed its origins to St Osmund, the second bishop of the diocese (1077-1099), who came to England with William the Conqueror: but this has been seriously questioned since no ascription of any liturgical regulations or innovations on his part can be traced before the 14th century. The opinion now prevailing is that Richard Poore, Dean of Salisbury from 1198 to 1215 and bishop of the diocese from 1218 to 1228, was the person most instrumental in the development of the Sarum Use. It would appear that under St Osmund, during whose episcopate the new cathedral of Old Sarum was completed in 1092, a constitution was drawn up for the governance of the cathedral and the regulation of its chapter. Then under Richard Poore, during whose episcopate the see was transferred from Old Sarum to New Sarum in the early 13th century, the clarifying, codifying, amplifying, and systematizing of liturgical practices was completed. Anything like the earliest definitive statement of the Sarum Use comes from customs of a religious house of Bishop Richard Poore, which is dated before 1220 because it contains the feast of the Martyrdom of St Thomas Becket; but not the feast of his Translation which was set in 1220'.

His Interest in the Education of the Young

Whilst Bishop of Salisbury he took an active interest in the religious education of children and endowed a number of bursaries for the children of poor local families. He decreed the clergy should not enjoy more than one benefice and should not be involved in any 'worldly business'. Poore House in Salisbury's Bishop Wordsworth's school, today, is named in memory of Richard's legacy to Salisbury schools.

His Palace

In the Close Rolls for 1221 there are two grants made by King Henry III to Bishop Poore of timber for the building of his palace, firstly, *'Grant of building materials. The King to Peter de Malo-Latu, health. Know that we have given to our venerable father Richard, Bishop of Salisbury, twenty couples (of beams) in our park of Gillingham to make his hall at New Sarum ......'* *Westminster 9 May 1221.* And, secondly, *'To John of Monmouth, health. We order you to let the venerable father Bp of Salisbury to have ten couples of oak in our wood at Milcet (ie Melchet, near Whiteparish) which we have given him to make his new chamber at Sarum. 30 December 1221'.*

Bishop Poore's own accommodation, his 'palace', is likely to have been the first of the cathedral houses to be completed on what became The Close around the new cathedral. It was built of stone some three hundred paces south east of the cathedral and would have been ready for occupation well before his translation to Durham in 1228. Its lower floor had an undercroft (54ft x 24ft) divided into bays, three in length and two in width which survive today. It was probably used for storage; and another large chamber to the south west, which was also probably used for storage. Both rooms were subject to flooding over the centuries. Upstairs is the Great Hall, or Aula, leading off to the bishop's quarters (the Solar or Camera). The weight of the Aula floor was carried on the stone ribs of the undercroft. These ribs spring from three low pillars. It would have had only the basic comforts.

The Great Hall would have been open to the rafters with an open fireplace of large stones in the middle. The bishop's table would have been on a dais and those 'seated below the salt' would have sat on wooden benches at long tables along the side walls which were painted with red flowers, green petals with curved stems: an arrangement typically seen in a great manor or a castle of the period. Today one wooden wall panel may be opened to reveal part of the original painting. The kitchen was possibly within a wooden building nearby; the Bishop's chapel would have led off from the Aula; and a larder or buttery, and a sewerey, where linen and small furniture would have been stored, would have been near the entry doors of the Aula. The layout would have been similar to the palace at Wells, built by Bishop Jocelin at the same time, but his was on a larger scale.

Succeeding bishops enlarged the palace, improved its facilities, employed a wide variety of architecture and made it warmer and much more comfortable inside. A chapel was added, a kitchen installed and an entrance hall was inserted into the north front. The result is an interesting assortment of country house architecture added on through the ages. There are also some good paintings to be found, mostly of the previous occupants, which adorn the reception rooms and main staircase.

In 1947 the bishop of the day, Geoffrey Lunt, decided that the palace was much too large and moved to Mompesson House (now a National Trust property) and, in 1951, moved to the South Canonry at the south east end of the Close. At about that time the Dean and Chapter decided to rent the grounds and buildings to Salisbury Cathedral School, which now has the responsibility, in addition to running an independent preparatory school, for the education of the two cathedral choirs (boys and girls). Additional main classrooms, laboratories, art and technology centres, a gymnasium, dormitories and a new pre-prep school have been added over the years. The Great Hall is now called the Big School Room, or BSR, and is the scene of school assemblies, lectures and musical evenings etc.

Elias de Dereham, Bishop Poore's Omnicompetent Designer of Salisbury Cathedral

Elias was born c. 1166 at West Dereham in Norfolk. He was a bright boy and soon came under the patronage of Hubert Walter, also a native of West Dereham, who was later to become Bishop of Salisbury (1189-94) and then Archbishop of Canterbury. Elias had been closely involved with building the new abbey at Dereham in 1188 and probably accompanied Hubert Walter to Salisbury. He was almost certainly a graduate of Paris University where he would have studied the arts, law and architecture earning the title of 'Master Elias'. Whilst in Paris he would have come to know Stephen Langton (later Archbishop of Canterbury), Richard Poore and Edmund Rich of Abingdon (later, also, Archbishop of Canterbury 1234 – 40 and Canonised) and many others who were to play leading roles in English state and church affairs. In 1201 he was appointed steward to Archbishop Hubert Walter in Canterbury, who died in 1205, and was the executor of his will as well as taking over all temporal affairs at Canterbury during the interregnum before the arrival of the new archbishop. He was appointed a Royal Clerk in 1205. At about this time he acquired the churches of Brightwalton and Melton Mowbray, gifts from the monks of Battle and Lewes, in Sussex.

Hubert Walter's death in 1205 forced Elias to transfer to the household of Bishop Jocelin of Wells, again as steward. With the imposition of the Papal interdict Jocelin and Elias went into exile in France together with Jocelin's brother, Bishop Hugh (St Hugh) of Lincoln. Hugh promoted Elias to the Lincoln Prebend of Laffard and in November 1212 appointed him executor of his will. The most important of Elias's contacts made in exile was Archbishop Stephen Langton. He was twice employed as Langton's Steward. In the next year he was given custody of Rochester Castle.

He goes into Exile

Following the sealing of Magna Carta in 1215, at which Elias was present and was probably responsible for overseeing its drafting, Elias was made a Commissioner for the Promulgation of the Charter and helped distribute at least ten copies around the shires. The Pope annulled the Charter a few weeks after it was sealed and suspended Stephen Langton who went into exile once more. Prince Louis, the Dauphin of France, accepted an invitation from the rebel barons to become their leader. He landed in England in May 1216. Elias soon became an enthusiastic adherent of the rebel barons and preached their cause at St Paul's Cross in London declaring that 'the Pope does not understand the situation in England'. King John died shortly after in 1216 and Prince Louis was compelled to return to France. Peace was restored in England but Elias was despoiled of his various properties and exiled to France. By 1220 he was pardoned and allowed to return to Langton's household and assisted in the design and construction of a splendid shrine to St Thomas Becket in Canterbury cathedral (the body of St Thomas was brought up from the crypt and installed in the east end of the cathedral. Bishop Richard Poore of Sarum was also involved in the consecration ceremony). Elias was described by the chronicler Matthew Paris as 'an incomparable artificer'.

Elias Returns to England to Live in Salisbury

It was inevitable that it would be to Elias de Durham that Bishop Poore and his Chapter would turn for architectural advice. Soon after his return to England, Bishop Richard Poore appointed him a Canon of Sarum Cathedral holding the Prebend of Beaminster Secunda. He also became a canon of Wells cathedral and was a great friend of Adam Locke, the Master Mason at Wells. Elias was one of many distinguished senior clerics who were invited to lay foundation stones during the ceremonies at New Sarum on 28 April 1220. He built and lived at Leaden Hall, a grand and beautiful canonical building in the newly created Close around the new cathedral, which he is likely to have designed as a model of what a canon's home should be.

He resided in Leaden Hall for the rest of his life; but, on his death, it was left to his executors and successors to dispose of the building and finish paying for its construction. The original building was pulled down in 1718, the little of what remained was destroyed in 1910, only the foundations and a brick wall are left. It is now the site of Leaden Hall Girls' School. Elias was in great demand elsewhere as well as his involvement with the decoration of the new cathedral in Salisbury. He worked at Westminster Hall and designed the tomb and effigy of Queen Joan of Scotland in the nunnery at Tarrant Crawford in Dorset, which was founded by Bishop Richard Poore in 1220, and he designed the King's Painted Chamber at Winchester Castle. He was an executor of the wills of three archbishops of Canterbury. Robert Bingham, who had been a Canon at Old Sarum before the move, succeeded Richard Poore as Bishop of Salisbury in 1229. He was very much a building bishop and took responsibility, with Elias and Nicholas of Ely, for continuing the building of the new cathedral without a break. Elias visited Durham cathedral and would have advised Bishop Poore on any improvements he intended to make in the cathedral (he was probably involved with the Chapel of the Nine Altars). He was appointed Bishop Poore's executor when he died. During his time in Salisbury he also found service with Peter des Roches, Bishop of Winchester, a political rival of both Archbishop Langton and Bishop Poore, and helped him found monastic houses in Selbourne and Titchfield and, eventually, acted as Peter's executor. He also held the peculiar of Harrow, the chancel of which church he was repairing in 1242.

The Rise and Fall of Clarendon Palace

Whilst the cathedral at Sarum was being built during the latter half of the 11th century, William the Conqueror started to build his palace on the site of an Anglo-Saxon hunting box in Clarendon forest. It soon became the centre of a vast royal hunting ground stretching from Windsor to Southampton.

King Henry III engaged Elias de Dereham as his designer for a much improved palace. From then on the royal palace became the centre of a huge playground for royalty, nobles, their wives and children. Government and the King's Court met frequently in the Great Hall and it was there that, in 1164, the *Constitutions of Clarendon and the Assize of Clarendon* were promulgated which, together with Magna Carta, became the birth pangs of freedom for the common man. The Longespées, Marshals and D'Evreux families would have been frequent visitors to Clarendon Palace. But over the next three centuries or so royal interest in the palace began to fade away as its occupants preferred the many advantages of a London base. In the 17th century King Charles I sold the palace and Charles II bought it back only to sell it on to Lord Chancellor Hyde, Earl of Clarendon (founder of the Oxford University Clarendon Press). The decline continued and it became a complete ruin. The good news is that in recent years some interesting research has been undertaken, the area has been cleared of undergrowth and the outline foundations of this great medieval palace are now accessible to visitors.

Master Elias de Dereham, now a canon of Salisbury and Wells and a successful Master of Law, Architecture and Building, had acquired fame and fortune. His was not a common achievement – priests tended to be strictly religious and sometimes political; it was left to tradesmen such as master masons to plan and build.

The remains of the Royal Palace at Clarendon 2010.

Nicholas of Ely was his Master Mason. Elias was a rich peaceful man. But he seems not to have been interested in promotion within the church and found great contentment in his splendid work in Salisbury, Canterbury, Winchester Cathedrals and many other places.

The Death of Elias in 1246

Elias de Dereham died in 1246 at the age of eighty – a very old age for those days. It was said that his longevity was due to a diet of vegetables. No one seems to know where Elias was buried. He is commemorated today by a statue on the southern side of the central crossing in Salisbury cathedral which was presented to the cathedral by the Freemasons. Elias is seen carrying a model of the cathedral.

Unfortunately Bishop Robert Bingham, Elias de Dereham and Nicholas of Ely died in 1246 and that year may be considered to be the end of the first building phase. The new phase started with the arrival from York Minster of King Henry III's nominee William of York, a distinguished judge with twenty years in the King's service. He was appointed Bishop of Salisbury (1247-57) and brought with him two experienced craftsmen Master Ralph of York who replaced Master Elias de Dereham and Master Nicholas of York who became Master of Works. Their work on the north nave transept roof is considered to be the finest surviving medieval roof in the country. Tim Tatton Brown, the much respected Archaeologist and Freelance Historian, notes that Close rolls correspond accurately with the dendrochronology showing that the work took place in the years 1251-53.

Bishop Poore's Translation to Durham Cathedral

Bishop Richard Poore was translated to Durham on 14 May 1228. His new episcopate was no sinecure. On arrival he found that the Cathedral Chapter was in turmoil over the appointment of a new Prior and matters had reached such a serious stage that members were sending strongly-worded complaints to the Papal Curia. Richard, no stranger to such matters, immediately set about a round of consultations and then worked out a detailed constitution which proved acceptable to the Chapter. It became the basis of church government in Durham until the 16th century.

Bishop Poore's Last Words

He died in Durham in 1237. His wish to be buried near his home in the Tarrant area, some 355 miles away, was granted. His last words quoted *Psalm 4, verse 9 'I will lay me down in peace and take my rest'*. His old friend in Paris and in Salisbury, Canon Elias de Dereham was his executor.

There are some doubts as to where Bishop Richard Poore was buried. The most likely place is Tarrant Crawford, some four miles from Blandford Forum, where there was a large flourishing Cistercian abbey and nunnery (both later dissolved by King Henry VIII in 1539 during the Reformation). Also buried in the abbey was Queen Joan, wife of King Alexander II of Scotland, daughter of King John and sister to King Henry III. She died in 1238. Two coffin lids, believed to have been those of Queen Joan and Bishop Richard, may be seen in the delightful little 12th century St. Mary's church, Tarrant Crawford, near the ruins of the abbey (St. Mary's church is now cared for by the Churches' Conservation Trust. It is usually open for visitors and has some impressive, but rather faded, medieval wall paintings dating to the 13th and 14th centuries).

St Margaret's Church, Tarrant Crawford, possible burial site of Bishop Richard Poore. Photograph by Christopher Dalton.

Matthew Paris, the chronicler, describes Bishop Richard Poore as 'a man of unparalleled piety and profound learning... It also redounds to his immortal praise, that he transferred the church of Salisbury... to a fitting situation and by the help of some famous architects, whom he had summoned from distant provinces.

Bishop Richard Poore's Palace Chapel, a Turning Point in British History

It is interesting to note that in 1688 Bishop Poore's chapel became the scene of a major turning-point in the history of Great Britain. The bishop at that time was Seth Ward, then an old man, growing increasingly senile and infirm. He left Salisbury to live quietly in semi-retirement (died 1689). What happened in his absence was one of the most dramatic incidents in the history of this palace.

King James II had upset public opinion by attempting to introduce unpopular toleration for all religious groups, including the Roman Catholics. Eventually a powerful clique of leading members of English society, and the Government, invited James II's Protestant son-in-law, Prince William of Orange (Stadtholder of the United Provinces in Holland) to invade England. William landed with a large army at Torbay on the 5th November 1688. James II hastened to Salisbury to make the city a base for his anti-invasion military operations. James was received by the citizens of Salisbury with a tumult of cheering through the city to the doors of the Bishop's palace.

The King's forces were concentrated at Warminster. John Churchill (later the Duke of Marlborough) was the Commander of the Royal Army. He invited the King to Warminster to inspect the troops massed there. However, unknown to James, Churchill had already decided, secretly, to change sides and was preparing to hand the King over to William of Orange.

While James II was at the palace a very nasty row developed. The King's Protestant chaplain, Dr Knightly Chetwood, arrived in the palace chapel to conduct a service. On arrival he found that the chapel was already occupied by several Roman Catholic priests intending to say Mass. Dr Chetwood demanded their withdrawal. If this was not done, he stated, he would resign his chaplaincy. James, after some hesitation, agreed and the Anglican service was performed in the chapel before a large and enthusiastic congregation. The soldiers present, who were the very men on whom the King was hoping to rely, declared that they would gladly lay down their lives for the King and the Church of England.

As James arrived at the door of the palace to enter the coach, which was to take him to Warminster, he had a severe nose-bleed. The King was led upstairs to his bedchamber (known today as the King's Room and, by a strange chance, is now the school's sick-bay) and was put under the care of a local 'chirurgeon'. The King had to rest there for three days. That three days' delay was fatal. One after another, James' leading supporters (including John Churchill and the English army) joined William of Orange. Realising that Salisbury was no longer safe, and that he was surrounded by traitors. King James returned post-haste to London on November 22nd to abdicate and, within a week, fled to France.

A fortnight after James' departure from Salisbury, William of Orange entered the City of Salisbury. He was received by the citizens with a tumult of cheering through the city to the doors of the Bishop's palace. William stayed for one night at the palace before proceeding to London to become King William III of England.

I am indebted to Peter Smith for the information on the Turning Point mentioned above.

Chapter Nine

William de Waude's Eye-Witness Account of the Cathedral's Transfer to New Sarum, Translated by William Dodsworth from the Latin in 1814. King Henry III Helps with the Finances. Building Statistics. The Bell Tower.

Author's Note: The following is a detailed account of the early building history of Salisbury Cathedral written by William de Waude, Precentor, then Dean of Sarum (elected 1220), translated from the Latin text by William Dodsworth, quondam head verger whose brother was the cathedral treasurer, and entitled *'An Historical Account of the Episcopal See and Cathedral Church of Sarum, or Salisbury'*. It was sold to the public from his house in Salisbury Cathedral Close during 1814.

William de Waude's Notes Dated Before 1217

In the time of Herbert, of happy memory, Bishop of Sarum the canons of the church held frequent consultations relative to its translation to a more free and convenient place. For, as it was surrounded by the walls of the king's fortifications, it was exposed to various troubles and continually laboured under the most grievous injuries and oppressions. By the diligence of this bishop, who was a person of great sagacity and able in temporal matters, the affair was so far advanced, that a plot of ground was selected, with general approbation, as a more commodious situation for the church, and as affording each of the canons a proper space for the erection of a dwelling-house. The design was favoured by the illustrious king of England, Richard, who freely gave his assent, but afterwards, the bishop, having composed the charges of finishing so great a work and materially considered his own ability to defray the expense, concluded that it would far exceed his utmost means, although he was rich and careful. Hence he proceeded no further in the project. Afterwards, in the reign of the most cruel King John, he suffered great losses in his goods and possessions; being stripped by confiscations, or what he had devoted to so pious a purpose. Truly, God knows whether this bishop was a man of sanguinary disposition, and not permitted to build the House of the Lord; and therefore this work devolved on his successor, who was of a most peaceable temper, but, by God's assistance, I will relate this matter, as it proceeded successfully in my time.

Author's Note: King Richard's assent given, perhaps, in 1194 shows that plans to transfer the cathedral away from Old Sarum were considered in some detail many years before they were approved by Pope Honorious in 1218. The long absences abroad of King Richard, lack of money, the Pope's interdict and King John's disastrous wars in France were certainly good reasons for the delay.

1217 Bishop Richard Poore is Translated to the See of Sarum

In the year of Grace, 1217, upon the death of Bishop Herbert shortly after that of King John, the affairs of the See of Rome in this kingdom were administered by Gualo, Cardinal Legate, then resident here, who carried matters with a high hand. Richard, Bishop of Chichester, the brother of Herbert, was at that point translated to the See of Sarum by the Pope's authority. The Legate was assiduously laboured to effect this translation; because Bishop Poore had been a useful assistant to him in managing the affairs of the realm. Therefore, after a report was transmitted to the Holy Roman See, the assent of the Pope was given.

1218 Bishop Richard Poore Petitions the Pope, who Grants Permission for the Cathedral to be Translated to New Sarum

The said Bishop, pitying the sufferings of the church of Sarum, which he had newly espoused, and being not a little solicitous for its liberation, joined with the dean and chapter, in the year of Grace 1218, in despatching special messengers to that city which is the mother and mistress of all. These agents represented the necessities of the church and the manifold inconveniences of its situation. They were charged, also, with letters from Gualo, the Legate, framed on an inquisition taken by him, concerning these matters, in virtue of a mandate from the Pope; and at length brought back an indulgence, granted by the bounty of the apostolic see, in this form.

'Honorious, Bishop, servant of the servants of God: to our reverend brother, Richard, bishop, and to our beloved sons, the dean and chapter of Sarum, health and apostolic benediction'.

'My sons, the dean and chapter: it has been heretofore alleged before us, in your behalf, that as your church is built within the fortifications of Sarum, it is subject to many inconveniences and oppressions, and you cannot abide therein without great corporal peril; for, being situated on a lofty place, it is continually shaken by the concussion of the wind; so that while you are celebrating the divine offices, you can scarcely hear each other. Besides, the persons resident there, suffer continual oppression, that they are scarcely able to keep in repair the roof of the church, which is often torn by tempests. They are also forced to buy water, at as great a price as would purchase the common drink of the country. Nor is there any access to the church, without leave of the castellans; so that it happens on Ash Wednesday, when the Lord's Supper is administered, at the same time of synods, and celebrations of orders, and on other solemn days, that the faithful, who are willing to visit the church, are refused entrance by the keepers of the castle, on the plea that the fortress is thereby endangered. Besides, as you have not dwellings sufficient for yourselves, you are compelled to rent houses of the laity. In consequence of these and other inconveniences many absent themselves from the service of the church'.

'We, therefore, to provide for this exigency, gave our letters and mandate to our beloved son, Gualo, Cardinal Presbyter of St Martin's and legate of the Apostolic See, diligently and carefully to enquire into this matter, either by himself, or others, as he should see expedient; and to make a faithful report to us. And whereas he has transmitted to us, under his seal, the depositions of witnesses, here upon received; we have caused the same to be inspected by our chaplain, who has found the representations before made, relevant to the aforesaid inconveniences, to be sufficiently proved. Therefore, the truth, by his faithful report, being evident, we do, by the authority of these presents, grant to you, free power to translate the said church to another more convenient place; but saving to every person, secular and ecclesiastical, his right, as well as reserving the dignities, and all the liberties of the church, in their full state and force. And it shall not be lawful for any person, in any manner, to infringe, or rashly to oppose this grant: otherwise, be it known, that he would incur the indignation of Almighty God, and of the Blessed Saints, Peter and Paul, his apostles. Dated at the Lateran, the fourth of the calends of April, in the second year of our pontific'.

1218 Continued. The Bishop Outlines Details of the Move to the Dean and Chapter and Explains the Finances.

Then the Bishop, earnestly exerting himself that the enterprise, which through the mercy of God had been begun, might be happily finished, without delay, caused all who were principally concerned in this matter, namely, being present, decreed in the following manner:

'To all the children of our holy mother church of Sarum, as well present as future to whom this writing shall come;

Richard, by divine permission, the humble servant of the church of Sarum; and Adam, the dean, and the chapter of Sarum, health in the Lord. Free power being granted to us by our most holy father, Pope Honorious, to translate the church of Sarum to a more commodious place, on account of the many inconveniences and oppressions under which it laboured, and of which sufficient proof hath been made before him, as in the proceeding Act, is more fully contained, we have caused a general convocation of the canons of Sarum, by themselves, for the major part, or by their proctors, being resident in chapter'.

'The virtues and inclinations of everyone being diligently examined, it was unanimously answered, that it was useful and convenient to translate the church to a more commodious place. And when the charges which the translation and construction of the new fabric required, were considered, (since a community can accomplish that effectually and speedily which a single person sometimes attempts in vain) they all and everyone promised, with a willing mind to assist in the building of the new fabric, according to their prebendal estates, continually for seven years, in the terms following. For the greatest security, a promissory act was drawn up and signed, stating what, and how much each would annually contribute'.

'We, all and singular, by this our present writing, both strengthened by the seal of the chapter, and corroborated by the subscription of each and everyone, to voluntary bind ourselves, and appoint by our common provision, four terms in which, during every year to the seventh, we will pay, without contradiction or fraud, the fourth part of the money annually promised to be applied towards the building, and, by the grace of god, the completion of our fabric. These are the terms: the first, on the Feast of All Saints; the second, on the Purification of the Blessed Virgin Mary; the third, on the Ascension of Our Lord; and the fourth, on Lammas Day. The payment of the said contribution is to be made in the Chapter House of Sarum at the terms specified, to such persons as shall be deputed for the purpose, on the part of the bishop and chapter. Done in the year of Incarnation 1218, in the second year of our pontificate, in the Chapter House of Sarum, on the day of the Saints Processus and Martinianus'.

Author's Note: This shows that the cathedral in Old Sarum had a chapter house, perhaps, a small and cramped one.

The same year, the bishop gave the precentorship to William de Waude, which Thomas de Disci before held. This was on the Advent of the Lord; on which day he was installed, the dean being absent.

1219 A Temporary Wooden Chapel and a Cemetery is Built on the New Site. A Local and National Plan for Fundraising is Agreed.

In the year of Grace 1219 a new wooden chapel was begun at New Sarum, in honour of the Blessed Virgin, on Monday next after close of Easter. In a short time the work was so far advanced, that on the Feast of the Holy Trinity, the lord bishop first celebrated divine service therein and consecrated the cemetery. The same year, being the third of his pontific, the chapter of Sarum assembled at the Feast of the Assumption, the bishop, dean, chanter, chancellor, and treasurer assisting. The canons present unanimously decreed that the translation from the old place to that of the new fabric, should be made on the Feast of All Saints, next following, by those who were willing and able, and others, in the meantime, were charged with the care of the building. They decreed also that the heirs of the first builders, as well as canons and vicars, should receive two parts of the just value of what should be actually built, the third part being yielded for the land. The appointment and collation of the houses, after the first vacancy, were to be left on sale to the bishop; but the family of the deceased person, who first built, or the persons to whom the said two parts were by him bequeathed, were to remain in possession of the houses until satisfaction was made for the price, according to his last will.

Author's Note: This new chapel, according to Rodney Maude in his History of St Thomas's Church, Salisbury, was a place of worship for all the men working on the site of the new cathedral. Soon after 1226 the original wooden building was superseded by a small stone church dedicated to St Thomas of Canterbury (Thomas Becket who was murdered in Canterbury Cathedral in 1170). This building had a nave and choir with north and south transepts but no side chapels, aisles, clearstoreys or tower. Various enlargements followed over the years.

It was also ordered that the contribution assigned for the use of the fabric should be paid at the four terms by each of the canons, in such manner, but having respect for the time of the receipts, everyone should answer for that portion which he received, as well as the living and the heirs of the deceased also canons and vicars and chaplains; and the vicar was to answer for the canon his principal. And it was decreed that such as should not pay the said portion, within eight days of the stipulated term, or should not have leave of delay, were to be apprised that they were suspended from entrance into the church, unless unavoidable accidents could be alleged in excuse. Also, on the death of any canon, all the appurtenances belonging to the land were to remain upon prebend, as well as fixtures.

But the Bishop, being still solicitous in his design, and perceiving that these sums were not sufficient to complete the work, by the advice of the chapter appointed preachers, or rather collectors of alms, through divers bishoprics in England. The clerks and inferior ministers all declining the office he addressed himself, with sighs and tears, to the higher persons. Some of them, likewise, excused themselves; but others cheerfully undertook the task, he gave them proper instructions. As the Nativity of the Lord drew near, they left the habitations which they had prepared for their use against the holidays and went abroad, everyone to the district assigned. W. the precentor, to the bishopric of London; Mr W de Badiston, to Canterbury; Mr R. de Hertford, to the bishopric of Ely; Mr H. the Chancellor, to the bishopric of Winchester; Mr. W de Wilton, to the bishopric of Exeter; Robert, the scot, to Scotland; Mr Luke, to the bishopric of Chichester. Others were afterwards, in like manner, dispersed through divers places. But, as to other matters relating to the church, during that year, few or none came to my knowledge; because I was long absent in the bishopric in London promoting the affairs of our establishment to the utmost of my power.

1220. The Foundation Stones are Laid. The King and Court are Unavoidably Absent: but a Multitude of Local People Attend including Earl William Longespée and his Wife the Countess Ela.

In the year of Grace 1220, on the day of St Vitalis the Martyr, which was then the fourth of the calends of May, the foundations of the new church of Sarum were laid. Now the bishop expected that our lord the king would have come hither, on that day, with the legate and the archbishop of Canterbury and many of the English nobility. Hence he prepared a solemn entertainment, at a great expense, for all who should appear; but in consequence of a negotiation then pending with the welsh, at Shrewsbury, he was disappointed, he could not, however, defer the ceremony because it had been publicly announced throughout the diocese.

On the day appointed, the bishop came with great devotion, few earls or barons of the country attended; but a great multitude of the common people crowded hither from all parts. Divine service was performed, the grace of the Holy Spirit invoked, and the bishop, putting off his shoes, went in procession with the clergy to the place of foundation, singing the Litany. After the Litany, a sermon was made to the people, and the bishop laid the first stone for Our Lord, Pope Honorious, who had granted leave to translate the church; the second, for the lord S (Stephen Langton) archbishop of Canterbury, and cardinal of the holy roman church, at that time with Our Lord the King in the marches of Wales. Then he added to the new fabric, a third stone, for himself. William Longespée, earl of Sarum, laid the fourth stone; and the fifth was laid by Ela née Vitri, Countess of Salisbury. After her, the few noblemen present added each a stone. Then Adam, the dean; W. the chantor; H. the chancellor; A. the treasurer; and the archdeacons and canons, who were present, did the same, amidst the acclamations of the multitude; the people weeping for joy, and contributing thereto, with a ready mind, according to their ability.

But, in process of time, the nobility being returned from Wales, several came hither, and each laid his stone, binding himself to some special contribution for the whole seven years.

1220 Continued. A New Dean and Other Officials are Appointed and the Building of the New City on the Same Site is Mentioned.

At the Feast of the Assumption, next following, in a general chapter, and in the presence of the bishop it was thus provided:

Any canon failing to pay what he had promised to the fabric, if his prebend was within the diocese of Sarum, someone should be sent, on the part of the bishop and chapter, fifteen days after the period had elapsed, to raise what was due from the corn which was found there. As long as such person should continue for that purpose, he was to be maintained, with all necessaries, from the goods from the said prebend. But if the prebend of the defaulter should be situated in any other bishopric, he was to be denounced as contumacious to that bishop, by the letters of the bishop and chapter, and was either to be suspended from entering the church, from celebration of divine service, or excommunicated, according to the chapter should judge proper.

And at the chapter then held which began on the morrow of the Assumption, and lasted three successive days, Adam, the dean, was present in good health. He hastened from hence to Sunning where he arrived on the octave of the Assumption. The morrow of the Vigil of St Bartholomew, the apostle, he died; and the third day following his body was brought to Sarum and honourably interred in the new chapel.

By mandate of the bishop, the chapter's letters were issued, citing all the canons then in England, to assemble at Sarum, on Sunday next after the Exultation of the Holy Cross and elect a dean. On that day, the bishop being present, about twenty seven canons appeared, of whom three were selected, secretly and singly, to take the votes of everyone in writing. Richard Grossa Testa, then archdeacon of Wiltshire, with two other canons, were appointed on behalf of all, to name the said examiners. They chose Mr Robert de Bingham, a man of great learning, and a long time in divinity; Mr Geoffrey de Rouen, who was then commencing in divinity at Paris; and Mr Henry de Bishopston, who used to read the Decretals at Oxford and then governed the schools in the new city of Salisbury. These people swore, on the Gospels, that they would fulfil their office without exception of persons and would designate a dean to be chosen by the majority.

Author's Note: At this point Dodsworth says that the building of the city must have been considerably advanced previous to the dedication of the new cathedral. Dodsworth also omitted from his translation part of de Waude's account when describing the contest which ensued for the office of dean, to which he himself was elected, principally by the interest of the bishop.

1225. Divine Service in Held in Part of the New Cathedral. A Festival Conference is held in the Sarum Cathedral Chapter House.

In the year of the Incarnation, 1225, the bishop, finding the new fabric, by God's assistance, sufficiently advanced for the performance of divine service, rejoiced exceedingly, since he had bestowed great pains and given much assistance in this work. He, therefore, commanded William, the dean, to cite all the canons to be present on the day of St Michael following, at the joyful solemnity of their mother church; that is to say, at the first celebration of divine service therein. He ordered also, that on the morrow of the Festival a conference should be held in the Chapter House, relative to the affairs of the church, pursuit to the citation of the dean and chapter. On that day the following canons were present:

The Lord Bishop, who is also a canon.

W. the dean, G. the chantor. Robert the chancellor. Edmund the treasurer.

Humphrey, archdeacon of Wiltshire. William archdeacon of Berkshire.

Hubert archdeacon of Dorsetshire. Martin de Patteshull.

Luke dean of St Martin's London. Hugh de Wells archdeacon of Bath.

Gilbert de Lacy. Mr Henry Teissun. Mr Henry de Bishopston.

Mr Luke de Winton. Mr Martin de Summa. Mr Richard de Brembla.

Mr Thomas de Ebelesburn. Mr Henry de St Edmund.

Mr Robert de Worth. Mr Geoffry of Devon. Hugh de Temple.

William de Leu. Robert Coteral. Peter Picot. Elias Redal.

The Abbot of Sherborne. Anastasius the subchantor.

Mr R de Bingham. Mr Roger de Sarum. Daniel de Longchamp. Elias de Dereham. Richard de Maupoder. Bartholomew de Rennes. Valentinus. Stephen de Tyssebury.

1225 Continued. Three New Altars are Consecrated and a Great Festival takes place.

On the fourth of the canons of October, namely the Vigil of St Michael, which happened on a Sunday, the bishop came in the morning and consecrated three altars. The first, in the east part, in honour of the holy and undivided Trinity and All Saints. On which henceforward the mass of the Blessed Virgin was to be sung every day. He offered, for the service of the said altar and for the daily service of the Blessed Virgin, two silver basins and two silver candlesticks which were bequeathed by the will of the noble lady Gundria de Warren to the church of Sarum. Morever he gave, from his own property, to the clerks who were to officiate at that mass, thirty marks of silver, yearly, until he had settled as much in certain rents; and ten marks yearly, to maintain lamps round the altar. He then dedicated another altar, in the north part of the church, in honour of St Peter, then prince of the

Apostles; and a third, in the south part, in honour of St Stephen, the proto-martyr, and the rest of the martyrs.

On the day of St Michael following, the lord bishop of Canterbury preached a service to the people who came in great numbers. Afterwards he went into the new church and solemnly celebrated divine service. The said festival was thus happily conducted, from the beginning to the end, without the least interruption or disturbance. The persons who were present besides the knights and barons were:

> S. archbishop of Canterbury. Henry archbishop of Dublin.
>
> Richard bishop of Durham. Joceline bishop of Bath.
>
> Ralph de Nevil bishop of Chichester. Benedict bishop of Rochester.
>
> The bishop of Evreux in Normandy who was, before, abbot of Bec.
>
> Richard bishop of Sarum.

Among these was Otto, the Pope's nuncio, who was come to intercede for one Falcarius, then in rebellion, having defended, against the king, his castle at Bedford. The nuncio was to have audience at Clarendon, on Michaelmas Day.

Author's Note: This seems to be an early reference to the Young King Henry III's royal palace at Clarendon which, today, is a ruin. Please see also page 81.

1225 Continued. King Henry III and Hubert de Burgh, Justiciar, Attend Mass and are Entertained at the Bishop's Palace.

On the Thursday following our lord the king and Hubert de Burgh, his Justiciar, came to the church. The king heard the mass of the glorious Virgin and offered ten marks of silver and one piece of silk. He granted also to the church the privilege of a yearly fair, from the Vigil to the Octave of the Assumption inclusive; namely, eight days complete. The same day the Justiciar made a vow that he would give a gold Text (Bible) with precious stones, and the relics of divers saints, in honour of the blessed Virgin, for the service of the new church. Afterwards the king went down, with many noblemen and knights, to the bishop's house where they were entertained.

Author's Note: The bishop's house or palace is the present site of Salisbury Cathedral's Choir School. For further details of the palace please see Chapter Eight.

The Friday following came Luke, dean of St Martin's London, and Thomas de Kent, clerks of the Justiciar, who brought the aforesaid Text, and offered it on the altar of the new fabric, on behalf of Hubert de Burgh. By the advice of the bishop and the canons present, it was ordered to be delivered to the treasurer to be kept: and the dean of Sarum was to be entrusted with one of the keys.

The Sunday following the bishop obtained leave that the new altar and chapel should remain in his custody for the whole seven years following; and that the oblations made there should be appropriated to the use of the fabric, except such as were given by the faithful for the perpetual ornament and honour of the church. He promised to execute a deed, stipulating that, after the expiration of the seven years, all things should return into the custody of the treasurer; and the oblations of all the altars be applied to the common use, according to the ancient custom of the church of Sarum. And also that those things which should have been offered to adorn the church should then be delivered up. All which the bishop now committed to the custody of Elias de Dereham, in whom he reposed the greatest confidence.

On the day of the Holy Innocents the king and his Justiciar came to Sarum. The king offered one gold ring with a precious stone, called a ruby, one piece of silk, and one gold cup, of the weight of ten marks. When mass was concluded he told the dean that he would have the stone which he had offered, and the gold of the ring, applied to adorn the Text, which the Justiciar had given. But as to the cup he gave no particular directions. The Justiciar caused the Text, which he had before given, to be brought and offered it, with great devotion, on the altar. They repaired to the bishop's house where they were honourably entertained.

Earl William Longespée Returns to Die at Home

On Saturday next after the Epiphany, the fourth of the ides of January, William Longespée , Earl of Sarum, after encountering many dangers by sea and land, returned from the Gascoigne, where he had resided almost a year, with Richard, the king's brother, for the defence of the city of Bourdeaux. The said earl came that day, after nine o'clock to Sarum, where he was received with great joy and with a procession from the new fabric. On the morrow he went to the king who was sick at Marlborough. Eight weeks after that day on which he had been received in procession, on Saturday the nones of March, this noble earl died in the castle of Sarum and was brought to New Sarum with many tears and great lamentations. The said hour of the day on which he had been received with great joy, being the eighth of the ides of March, he was honourably interred in the new church of the blessed Virgin. At his funeral were present the bishops of Sarum, Winchester and some bishops from Ireland, Earl William Marshal, and Earl William de Mandville and these barons, Robert de Vieuxpont, Hugh de Gurnay, Ralph de Toani, with a great multitude of their military attendants.

1226 The Three Bishops are Translated from Old to New Sarum

In the year 1226, on the feast of Trinity, which then was the eighteenth of the calends of July, the bodies of three bishops were translated from the castle of Sarum to the new fabric, namely, the body of the blessed Osmund, the body of bishop Roger, and the body of bishop Joceline.

Author's Note: Their effigies and their tombs were brought down to the new cathedral where they were buried in the Trinity Chapel.

Here William de Waude's account comes to an abrupt end.

King Henry III's Role in Confirming and Financing the Move and the Subsequent Construction of the New Cathedral. Two Documents are Quoted.

Document No CLVII (pages 175-178) 30 January 1227 in the Medieval Source book/ORB Main Page/Linking other Medieval Sites.

Henry, by the grace of God King of England, Lord of Ireland, Duke of Normandy and Aquitaine and Count of Anjou, to his archbishops, bishops, abbots, priors, counts (earls), barons, viscounts, provosts, ministers and all bailiffs and vassals; health and greetings.

You know that we, out of reverence and honour for God and the Blessed Mary .... conceded and with the present charter confirmed to God, to the church of St Mary whose translation from our castle of Salisbury to a lesser place we hold correct, and at whose foundation we laid the first stone ... we want and concede for us and for our heirs that the place which is called A New Sarum shall be a free city in perpetuity with fortified enclosures ... and that the citizens of this town living there should be quit throughout the entire realm of commerce-duties, bridge-tolls, other tolls, lastage, stallage (dues paid for stalls in a market), cartage service ... and we confirm that the said citizens shall have in perpetuity the same liberties and exemptions throughout our entire kingdom as do the citizens of Winchester.

We wish to concede that the aforesaid bishop and his successors should enclose the aforesaid city of New Sarum with stout walls because of the fear of thieves and that they should hold the city as part of their own lordship ... we shall concede to the bishop and to his successors ... that they shall create, shift and alter the roads and bridges leading to the city as they think fit...

Document No CCVIII (pp 180-182) of 23 March 1227 of the same source book

We (have) conceded ... to the venerable father Richard, bishop of the same city, and to his successors, all the amercements (discretionary penalties and fines) from all the men, land and fiefs of the same bishop and from the dean and all the canons of the church of Salisbury and (the amercements) of all their men, lands and fiefs; namely, (we grant) the amercements which would have pertained to us, our heirs or to our viscounts, constables and bailiffs, if we had not granted them to the bishop and his successors. We conceded and, with the present charter, confirmed all these aforesaid (and other) liberties, free customs and exemptions on the part of ourselves and our heirs to God, to the church of St Mary of New Sarum, and to the aforesaid bishop and his successors as free, pure, and perpetual alms. For which reason we desire and firmly command that they shall thus have and hold them in perpetuity, and that the aforesaid dean and canons of Sarum and their successors, and all the men, lands, and fiefs of the bishop and all the men of those fiefs shall have the aforesaid liberties and free customs and exemptions absolutely and freely, wholly and completely, in all places and things, just as has been written above.

They may also have a fair at Sonning, at Wokingham (Berkshire) all the days of March; also at Ramsbury (Wiltshire) through March, with all liberties and free customs pertaining to markets of this sort.

Author's Note: Unfortunately, today, the monarch is no longer able to collect and receive money from these lucrative sources and dispose of it at will.

Some Building Facts and Figures

In his seminal book, entitled Salisbury Cathedral, originally published by Unwin Hyman in 1987, Roy Spring then Salisbury Cathedral's Clerk of Works, notes that after forty six years of continuous building from c.1220-1266 some 60,000 tons of stone were extracted from the mines at Chilmark and transported the twelve miles to Salisbury every year from March to October. Ten cart loads arrived each day on site together with security guards. The roofs of the cathedral, says Spring, contain approximately 2,800 tons of timber, 300 tons of lead were used to cover them and glaziers filled three quarters of an acre of windows with stained glass or grisaille glass. The depth of the cathedral foundations is 4.5 ft or 1.4 metres.

Author's Note: If the depth of the cathedral's foundation really was only 4.5 ft, then of course the four great central pillars at the centre crossing would have collapsed with the extra weight of the tower and the spire. However, it was already widely known that there was a raft of impacted flint gravel four feet below the surface of the field. This enabled the builders to sink the foundations a further 27 feet, thus avoiding, perhaps, a disaster of Venetian campanile proportions.

The roofs of the cathedral contain approximately 2,800 tons of timber, 400 hundred tons of lead were used to cover the roofs.

Roy Spring continues 'One of those present at the laying of the foundation stones in 1220 was Lady Alice Brewer who undertook to help the building work. She owned the manor of Worth Matravers in South Dorset and many limestone quarries at Downshay. It was from these quarries that she pledged a gift of limestone to cover the first twelve years of the building work. Today the cathedral contains a great deal of this limestone (also called shelly limestone as it contains 'unios' which are millions of years old insects trapped inside the stone) and, because it takes a high polish and is most attractive, it has been termed marble. The mines at Downshay produced some 12,000 tons of this shelly limestone for Salisbury Cathedral, all of which found its way from Poole Harbour to Christchurch then up the Avon River to Salisbury. Shelly limestone is still being mined today.

These are only some of the materials used during the first forty six years of building work. Such quantities mean little until one realises the physical and mental effort required to convert the stone, wood, lead and glass into a fit state for inclusion in the building. To ensure a continuous supply of material, the efficient collection and allocation of money, the recruitment of suitable craftsmen, all this would have called for leaders with authority and a determination to produce a beautiful house of prayer.

The Bell-Tower

A magnificent detached bell-tower, two hundred feet high with up to ten heavy and expensive bells, was also built mid-way between the new city and its cathedral sometime during the period 1230-60. Roy Spring notes that in 1645 the tower was captured by a Parliamentarian force under Colonel Ludlow and used as a guardroom and observation post to house a captured royalist commander and a number of royalist prisoners. A royalist company set out to rescue them and, on arrival, compelled an itinerant charcoal burner to place his load of charcoal next to the tower door and set it alight. This forced the Parliamentarian garrison in the tower, comprising five officers, eighty men together with one hundred and fifty horses, to surrender. In subsequent years the bells deteriorated and the tower became a disreputable ale house. The bell-tower and a tenement beside it were sold for £500 in 1790; all that remains today are a few brown marks on the grass in the summer months.

Chapter Ten

Some Comments on the Earlier Architectural Styles of Salisbury Cathedral e.g. Gothic, Early English Gothic and Episcopal. A Summary and a Comment.

The Gothic Style

Dictionaries define Gothic as a style of architecture and art which originated in the Middle East and was first introduced into Western Europe after the First Crusade and the capture of Jerusalem in 1099. Its prevalent features included the pointed arch, the rib-vault supported by buttresses, traceried windows and clustered pillars.

One of the early French builders to incorporate the pointed arch in his church architecture was the Abbe Suger during his reconstruction of part of the great cathedral of St Denis 1136-45, where the French kings were buried until the abolition of the monarchy. He was a member of the Cluniac branch of the Benedictines who took no special vow of poverty; and so he believed in the majesty of heaven in his structures, worthy of every embellishment such as sumptuous stained glass windows in St Denis, Notre Dame and Chartres cathedrals.

The great preacher, St Bernard of Clairvaux (1090-1153), was the leader of the reforming Cistercians who were the second great religious organisation to introduce Gothic architecture into France. He espoused a return to Christian simplicity, a vow of poverty and an end to extreme church ostentation. He was opposed to anything which detracted from the union of the soul with God; as shown, later, by the Cistercian decree of 1188 which ordered the removal of stained glass from churches and their replacement by grisaille glass – so familiar in much of the early fenestration of the new cathedral building in Salisbury, many examples are now elegantly displayed in the south east transept. St Bernard wrote

> *'You will find something more in woods than in books. Trees and stones will teach you that which you cannot learn from masters'.*

Prior to the Gothic 'revolution' in France, a great many Christian churches were based on Roman basilicas (from the Greek, basilikon, meaning royal, a palace of the king: later, a Latin word meaning a large oblong hall with double colonnades and a semi-circular apse, used for Roman courts of law and public assemblies), which were taken over as ready-made churches by the Christians. An ante-room at the western end of the basilica became a narthex (from the Greek) for use by adults who had not yet been baptised as Christians. Those wishing to join the Christian religion, called catechumens, needed instruction before they could be admitted as full members of the church. They could only attend the first

The SW Prospect of Salisbury Cathedral by J Harris (pre 1715) showing the Belfry Tower on the left and the Library Range adjoining the South transept.

part of the service; Holy Communion was reserved for the faithful. Thus the position of the font for baptism had to be near the inner doors of the narthex to enable the catechumens to be baptised in due course and then to take their places among the faithful. As the Christian religion spread, infant baptism became the practice and so the narthex soon became superfluous – and that is how the west front of a cathedral took the place of the narthex and became a major attractive characteristic of Gothic architecture.

The west front of Salisbury cathedral (so beautifully depicted by the Salisbury Guild of Embroiders in their wonderful tapestry now hanging from one of the four great central pillars at the cathedral crossing) has five tiers of statues – angels; patriarchs and prophets; apostles; virgins and martyrs and, finally, doctors and worthies of the church including Bishop Richard Poore (holding a model of his cathedral), St Osmund and King Henry III. But this is not all. Behind the lowest tier is a passage way to accommodate some members of the choir who could sing through a large hole behind some statues at that level.

Imagine, if you will, joining an expectant throng of Salisbury citizens sitting on the grass on a cool medieval summer evening at the foot of the west front of the cathedral, a beaker of mead in your hand, and excited chatter round about. As the sun goes over the horizon flares are lit which cast a golden glow over the medieval stone walls of the west front of the cathedral. Suddenly, drums are heard from above the statues; bugles sound, then a moment of utter silence until, to your amazement, the hidden choirboys behind the statues began to sing the '*Te Deum Laudamus*':

'To Thee all angels cry aloud the heavens and all the powers therein
To Thee cherubim and seraphim, continually to cry
Holy, Holy, Holy Lord God of Sabaoth:
Heaven and Earth are full of the majesty of Thy glory.
The glorious company of the apostles praise Thee
The goodly fellowship of the prophets praise Thee,
The noble army of martyrs praise Thee
And the Holy Church throughout the whole world doth acknowledge Thee'.

Another significant influence on the Gothic architecture sweeping across England came from the cathedral church at Sens in Burgundy where building began in 1130 and was completed by 1164. Sens was then an archbishopric of an immense province that included both Chartres and Paris. Pope Alexander III went into exile there in 1163 and so did Thomas Becket, who lived in exile at Sens from 1165-70 during his disagreement with Henry II (one of the chapels at Sens is dedicated to Thomas Becket wearing an enormous alb (long white vestment) which, today, has a place of honour among that cathedral's treasures). In 1174, when the choir of Canterbury cathedral burnt down, it was to the Sens architect that the Canterbury cathedral community turned for a replacement 'in the new Gothic style' says the late Laurence O'Keeffe, cathedral guide and knowledgeable historian.

Early English Style

It seems, therefore, that the Early English Gothic style developed from the French Gothic styles. Not perhaps so gaudy, grandiose and expensive as the Abbe Suger would have introduced: but not so plain as the Cistercians might have insisted. After all the planners of Old and New Sarum cathedrals were secular in outlook and practice; and they would have carefully examined what was available and deliberately chosen what they considered to be the most appropriate, useful and in line with all aspects of the Sarum Use. They had also to bear in mind their long outstanding intention of achieving the canonisation of the Blessed Osmund and the subsequent planning of his shrine in the cathedral. Moreover the actual decorations of the cathedral would have been supervised and/or carried out by those two highly respected and experienced English experts in their fields – Canon Elias de Dereham and Nicholas of Ely, the head mason. Amiens' cathedral was built more or less at the same time as Salisbury's and its design and contents probably retain, today, some of what Salisbury cathedral might have looked like in the first days of its Early English Gothic style.

As time went by, and more and more European cathedrals were being built or enlarged, so the Gothic style progressed – with almost every cathedral differing in detail. New ideas began to replace the Gothic style. Luther's Reformation, King Henry VIII's dissolution of the monasteries and his abolition of a great many chantry chapels dedicated to the souls of their founders, the rise and fall of Puritanism and, of course, the Romantic Gothic(k) Revival of the Victorian Age, all of which, over the centuries, swept away so much of the Early English Gothic style. The many valuable treasures donated by royalty, and the very rich, and often on public display, began to disappear without trace; the only evidence of their presence being lengthy inventories gathering dust in ancient libraries. (One recalls James Wyatt's destructive activities in Salisbury Cathedral in the late 18th century – according to local newspapers these were welcomed at the time: but reviled later).

The Episcopal Style in the Early 13th Century

The historian Virginia Jansen's paper delivered to the 1991 British Archaeological Association's Conference in Salisbury contained interesting and constructive comments on the phrase 'Episcopal Style' in relation to the construction of Salisbury Cathedral in the 13th century. She drew attention to the widespread effects of Pope Innocent III's interdict over England 1208-13; King John's subsequent submission to the Pope; and, most important of all, Stephen Langton's appointment as Archbishop of Canterbury. Shortly after that came the 4th Lateran Council in Rome of 1215 organised by the Pope and attended by the Church's hierarchy from all over Western Europe, including Stephen Langton and Richard Poore in the English delegation, which heralded a re-birth of the 'Universal Church'. The English delegates would have been inspired and full of energy and enthusiasm. But they could not have foreseen the sudden death of King John in 1216; peace restored throughout the land in 1217; a young boy on the throne of England advised by a competent and sympathetic Regency Council; and, of course, the Pope's agreement to issue a licence to transfer the cathedral away from its dreadful position at Old Sarum. All their long-held dreams were realised; and so, at last, the way was clear for Bishop Richard Poore and his Chapter to develop with flair and determination their previous outline plans into what became the Episcopal Style.

The Episcopal Style was introduced into other ecclesiastical buildings in England, suitably adapted to local conditions, the acquisition of sufficient finance and the need to balance existing structures. In Salisbury, however, the bishop had a free hand from the beginning and he was able to recruit the very best of designers, masons, other craftsmen and, with some initial difficulty, a large number of fundraisers. Moreover the Bishop was a member of his Chapter and had wide experience gained from his service as Dean of Sarum. The two really important designers of his church were Elias de Dereham and Nicholas of Ely, both of whom could be relied upon to recruit intelligent and enthusiastic members of the building team. Similarly, the availability of patrons such as the young king, his court, Archbishop Stephen Langton, wealthy merchants and local land owners could be relied upon for financial contributions of cash and kind such as wood, stone, Purbeck marble, lead etc.

Virginia Jansen notes 'Salisbury Cathedral was, perhaps, meant to be seen as an 'exemplum' of the New Universal Church, as Archbishop Stephen Langton, Richard Poore and others were formulating it both before and after the 4th Lateran Council. Salisbury Cathedral was removed from its secular surroundings and the bustle of a market town ... to its previously marked off site, encircled by its officials' houses, was rendered isolated and clearly visible in its even, regulated magnificence. The tone of reticence in relation to other English Gothic cathedrals is symptomatic of the 13th century episcopal reform and of efforts to administer church dioceses more rigorously and regularly. The controlled balance between cathedral grandeur and ordered simplicity ensures that at Salisbury the church maintained a due sense of decorum as a model cathedral of the reform movement; this ideal may be attributed to the mission of Bishop Poore and the men with whom he was associated. Poore's Use of Sarum, drawn up in 1213-14, is surely connected to the regular layout of the ground plan'. Virginia goes on to say:

'While Poore was in Paris both as a student and teacher of theology, he would certainly have been exposed to Peter the Chanter's remarks about the extravagance of church building. Peter was probably Langton's teacher and Langton was Richard Poore's. Poore and Langton remained in communication. Further, Salisbury's apparently chaste appearance may have reduced decorative Englishness in order to represent the new order of the Universal Church. During the interdict Langton stayed for a time in exile at the Cistercian abbey of Pontigny. Surely he would have noticed the simplified nature of Cistercian architecture about which he may have made comments to Poore in discussing church reforms. The abundant use of grisaille glass at Salisbury may reflect ascetic attitudes in these Episcopal as well as in Cistercian circles. The Gothic architecture of the cathedral looks more simplified than English, especially by the early 13th century as seen at Chartres or Soissons. While Poore and Langton stayed in Paris and France they may have been visually attentive enough to be able to transmit a feature such as quadripartite vaults'.

Sarah Brown notes that 'the Jesse Tree fragments now in the south aisle of the nave would have fitted both physically and iconographically into the east window of the Trinity Chapel which was, de facto, a Lady Chapel and the site of the daily Mass of the Virgin, although, by the end of the 18th century the glass had been moved first into the north transept and then into the nave. A Jesse window, depicting in visual terms the ancestry of Christ, had become a standard subject in the great churches of the 12th and 13th centuries'.

Also dating from the 13th century is the medallion of the martyrdom of St Stephen removed to the parish church of Grateley in Hampshire in the 18th century, which is attributed by Sarah Brown to the window above Salisbury Cathedral's altar of St Stephen dedicated in 1225.

Summary and Comment

The architectural style of Salisbury Cathedral during the 13th century seems to have been a mixture of French and Early English Gothic (Abbe Suger et al) as mitigated by Cistercian asceticism (St Bernard of Clairvaux) and, especially, by the Episcopal Style (Bishop Poore and his friends and advisors) and implemented within the overall plan by experienced chosen craftsmen.

Bill Bryson Hon. OBE (born Iowa, USA, 1951. Prolific travel writer), comments 'there is no doubt in my mind that Salisbury Cathedral is the single most beautiful structure in England, and the Close around it the most beautiful place'.

George Herbert, Rector of Bemerton, poet, d. 1633, had this to say in retrospect

'Lord, how can man preach the eternal word?
He is a brittle crazy glass: yet in thy temple though dost him afford
This glorious and transcendent place, to be a window, through thy grace'

Chapter Eleven

The Use of Grisaille Glass, Handmade Encaustic Tiles. A Hydrus. The Choir Stalls. Medieval Pigments for Painting and Writing. The Beautiful Chapter House and its Amazing Frieze (Stone Carvings). Green Men. The Three Heads of St John the Baptist. Daniel Defoe's Description of Salisbury Cathedral. Dean Ralph Brideoake's Prayer Desk

Grisaille Glass and Handmade Encaustic Tiles

One of the greatest glories of Salisbury cathedral is the large quantity of 13th century grisaille glass which has survived. The largest amount, now assembled in the fenestration of the south east transept, represents one of the most extensive and important collections in England.

Further enrichment of the eastern arm was provided by pavements of two-colour tiles arranged in geometric patterns. The pavement of the choir, into which several brasses and ledger stones had been set by the end of the Middle Ages, disappeared as a result of 17th century repaving that accompanied the refurbishment of the choir during Bishop Ward's episcopacy (1667-89). The original effect of these long-lost pavements can be appreciated from the closely related Clarendon Palace pavement preserved in the British Museum and from the surviving pavement still in situ in the choir practice room in the cathedral. The unpolished tiles now laid in St Peter's chapel, towards the east end of Salisbury Cathedral, were originally in the chapter house and are of the 13th century. Sarah Brown considers that as many as ten individual decorative elements can be identified. They were employed in an elaborate geometric web, each zone of pattern separated from the next by decorative fillets and, in this respect, the Salisbury cathedral pavements were richer even than the Clarendon Palace ones.

Handmade encaustic tiles originally laid in Chapter House. Now in St Peter's Chapel in Salisbury Cathedral c. 1265.

Salisbury Cathedral's Hydrus

From the time Salisbury Cathedral was being built, carpenters and masons obviously enjoyed carving splendid animals, birds, human heads (probably modelled from the citizens of Salisbury) and flowers. There is an abundance of them – especially in the chapter house. One of the more unusual carvings is that of a hydrus – a water snake, carved in Purbeck marble, in the 19th century and probably copied from a 13th century original. It is depicted slipping into the mouth of a crocodile-like creature, sliding down its throat, splitting the sides of its prey and emerging from its tail. On examination of other hydrus 'resurrection' depictions elsewhere, it seems that the hydrus (representing a human

Salisbury Cathedral's Hydrus c. 1860, after a medieval original.

being) enters the body of a crocodile (representing Hell or Hades) then, having been cleansed of worldly sins, emerges from the body and passes on up to Heaven. Another unattributed explanation states that the crocodile signifies Hell and the hydrus Christ, who descended into Hell to recover imprisoned souls … and then returns to Heaven. Today, not a lot of people have discovered the whereabouts of Salisbury Cathedral's hydrus – a challenge, perhaps, for the reader.

The Choir Stalls

In attempting to recreate the lost décor of the cathedral's 13th century interior it is easy to overlook one of its functionally most important aspects, namely the choir stalls, which survive in situ and virtually intact. Ignored in the earliest literature on the subject they have recently been identified by modern historians as the earliest complete set to survive in England. The choir of the cathedral church at Old Sarum is thought to have been furnished only with benches *(Hope 1917b, II5-6)*. According to Matthew Paris the new cathedral was provided with substantial stalls and desks during the episcopate of Bishop Bingham (1229-46). Sarah Brown notes 'the choir furniture shares many of the motifs of the surrounding architecture and the stalls are relatively plain, perhaps explaining why they have escaped scholarly notice for so long. The seats of the dignitaries and the stall ends are embellished with small quantities of ornament, including human heads (e.g. the elbow of the precentor's seat) and a variety of animals, too, although the bulk of the ornament is foliate, reminiscent of the architectural capitals and roof bosses. The stalls did not originally support canopies, as they do today, but were simply backed by the stone screens that enclosed the choir and separated it from the aisles'.

Medieval Pigments for Painting and Writing

The late Master Printer Partridge states 'tempora, using a gum and albumin (white of egg) medium, would have been used for wall and ceiling painting until the 15th century when oil based paints and inks were introduced. Earthy pigments like ochre for yellow and red, umber and iron oxide for rich browns, and vegetable colourings like madder were also used in the red-brown range. The blues may have come from another vegetable dye, indigo, or powdered lapis lazuli. These and other pigments were all used in the making of inks for illuminated manuscripts. There were two main recipes for writing inks in the medieval period. The more common one used oak galls (oak apples) and iron ferrite in a gum-water medium. The alternative used soot, or lamp black, in water, again with gum, fish glue or albumin as the bonding agent. Carbon inks were not generally used for legal documents as they had a tendency to flake off when subject to much handling. It is probable, therefore, that the Magna Carta is written using a water-based ink made from oak galls, iron ferrite and gum or albumin. Other pigments used for writing on vellum or parchment were, and probably still are, red lead, white lead, verdigris, yellow arsenic sulphide, red from crushed spiders (carmine), woad from plants, powdered gold and gold leaf'.

Salisbury Cathedral Chapter House

Conservation work on the west front of the cathedral, and some interesting dendrochronological investigations within the spire and elsewhere, have given archaeologists and historians opportunities to re-examine new evidence and to revise their opinions concerning the early days of the cathedral.

The building of the cloisters and the chapter house clearly were not after-thoughts tacked on after the first phase was completed in 1258. The cathedral in Old Sarum had its own administration area and its own secular cloisters, its clerical inhabitants were used to these, and the bishop found they provided a fair weather passage for him to walk to the cathedral in inclement weather. All concerned would, most certainly, have insisted on them in the early planning of the new cathedral for liturgical reasons. Chapter membership was increased from forty two, before the move to the new site, to fifty two by 1226.

However not all the clergy were happy with the result. Tatton-Brown says 'there is evidence to show that soon after these cloisters were completed, it was decided to enlarge them significantly; and that the bishop himself gave the extra land for this purpose to the Dean and Chapter. The main reason for this significant and grand enlargement was to allow a stone roof to replace the wooden roof originally installed along the cloisters – an exceptionally daring and expensive project. The widening of the cloister from about eight feet to eighteen feet enabled the stone roof to be built: but it also became necessary to strengthen the side walls. Nevertheless, it served its purpose, pleased the clergy and is the largest cloister in England'.

Sarah Brown, historian and source, says her research showed the chapter house was completed in the mid-1260s, it was an up-to-date, forward looking 'with-it' building very much in keeping with its time and the many fashions emerging from Henry III's magnificent new cathedral in Westminster, and from his recently completed palace at nearby Clarendon. A later date for completion would have missed these new fashions sweeping across the country during the early days of Henry III's reign. Hard evidence of this date includes concurrent work proceeding in the cathedrals of Westminster and Wells, the detailed sculptures on the Salisbury pulpitum which divided the nave from the choir (dated to the middle 1230s, removed by James Wyatt in the late 18th century and now incorporated in the Morning Chapel), the canopy and other details on the tomb of Bishop Giles de Bridport (in the east end of the south aisle) who died in 1262; but who may well have planned or approved the design before his death. In Dr Rodwell's opinion the cloisters and the chapter house were probably completed by 1266.

When the chapter house was completed, the lancet windows contained the heraldic stained glass shields of many famous local 13th century families. Most of these were destroyed in the following centuries. But early 19th century restoration rescued some which were reinstated at the foot of the restored great west front window of the cathedral. These are, reading from the left as you look up at the window from the nave:

1. **Shield of Gilbert de Clare.** Earl of Gloucester. Friend of the Royal Family.

2. A composite shield with a Byzantine border, the field having been made up of original fragments including a demon or dragon, or a monkey.

3. **Shield of Count Berengar's family of Provence France.**

4. **Shield of King Louis IX of France.** Leader of the disastrous 7th Crusade 1248 - 54. Died 1267. Later Canonised c. 1298.

5. **Shield of King Henry III of England** displaying the three ancient Lions of England. Died 1272.

6. **Shield of Richard, Earl of Cornwall.** King of the Romans. Younger brother of King Henry III; and

7. **Shield of Richard Bigod,** Earl of Norfolk and Earl Marshal.

It was the custom by the 13th century to honour great men and their families, especially those who provided cash or kind to a cathedral such as Salisbury, by inserting their shields, often in pairs, in the fenestration of a cathedral or its chapter house. Henry III and his family group, and members of his social circle, appear in Westminster Abbey and York Minster and it is likely that they would have been inserted in their lifetime (Henry III died in 1272, weak and senile, having never fully recovered from his capture by Simon de Montfort at the Battle of Lewes in 1264).

The chapter house was a most attractive secular room in which to conduct the administration of the diocese; and to entertain the king, his court and influential visitors from home and abroad. It provided a surprising contrast to the inside of the cathedral which, though painted too, was rather more subdued. The frieze was gilded and painted, the chapter house stalls were richly painted to give the impression of coloured damask curtains. The raised stalls for the senior clergy, at the eastern end, were unique marks of dignity as were the accompanying additional slender columns of Purbeck marble.

Earlier bishops would have played a major role in running the cathedral together with the Dean and assisted by the Canons Precentor, Chancellor and Treasurer, sometimes with co-opted members of the chapter or professionals. The Greater Chapter, comprising up to fifty two members, was responsible for the regular maintenance of the buildings and the performance of the liturgy. Later bishops, as holders of the prebend of Potterne, were entitled to attend meetings of the chapter, if they wished, and could act as Visitors settling internal church disagreement. The word chapter derives from the Latin word 'caput' meaning 'head' of which 'capitulum' or 'little head' is the diminutive. The Latin expression 'Ire ad capitulum' meant to attend a meeting at which members of the chapter would read a chapter of their rule (St. Benedict's) in a monastic cathedral, or a portion of scripture in a secular cathedral, after which the secular or liturgical business of the day would follow. (Archbishop Stephen Langton, arguably the greatest of the English medieval bishops, former Chancellor of the University of Paris and a personal friend of the powerful Pope Innocent III, is credited with the reorganisation of the Bible into chapters; thus it is reasonable to suppose that from the early 13th century a chapter of the Bible could have also been read, sometimes, prior to secular discussion). There are chapter houses in Westminster Abbey (built in the years 1250 to 1253), Wells, Exeter, Lincoln, York, Hereford, Chichester, Worcester, and Litchfield cathedrals. There are other chapter houses in other cathedrals and religious buildings. Those in Old St.Paul's and Beverley, Yorkshire have since been destroyed.

The chapter used to meet at mid-day in medieval times and occasionally after Prime following Lady Mass in the morning, if there was a long agenda. Subjects for discussion might have been:

a) Plans for visits by the king or other important people.

b) Weekly funding.

c) Election, rejection and selection of candidates for all sorts of appointments.

d) The administration of the diocesan establishments within and without the Close often involving endless discussions on maintenance.

e) The affairs of its schools and the Valley College (from its inception in 1260 to its winding-up in 1540) make frequent appearances on the agenda. It was situated between what is now De Vaux Place and the north bank of the river Avon. See also Appendix II.

f) The resident members of the Greater Chapter, and the choristers and vicars choral met daily in the chapter house to discuss business and to draw up the next day's readings etc.

g) Reports and progress of lawsuits and litigation generally; and

h) The hearing of petitions.

The chapter house is octagonal and has an internal diameter of 58 feet and a height of 52 feet. The roof is supported by a dramatic slender octagonal central column of purbeck marble with detached shafts and a moulded base below. It was restored in the 1850s under the direction of Henry Clutton 1819 - 1893. The popular satirical story of Reynard the Fox (which may have originated in Paris around 1200) appears to have been re-sculpted during the 19th century restorations. (A personal note. As a Steward/Guide of the Chapter House, I have learned the Japanese names of animals appearing at the foot of the central column of the chapter house. I use them to entertain Japanese parents and especially their young children who, otherwise, would sit bored stiff with expressionless faces on the stone seats). The restored chapter house became a memorial to Bishop Denison who died in 1854. He is buried between his two wives under the cedar trees in the cloister garth.

Henry Clutton, who was appointed architect responsible for major repairs of the cathedral, was trained in part by Decimus Burton and his architectural career included several country houses and London churches of which the Catholic church in Farm Street, Mayfair, is perhaps the best known. The Clutton family records note that his first real success was to have his plans for major repairs to Lille cathedral accepted by the Bishop in preference to those of French competitors. Having received the offer, he felt it only right to reveal to the Bishop that he was a Protestant, whereupon the Bishop withdrew the commission. How ironical it was that, when completing his work on the Salisbury Chapter House, he informed Bishop Kerr Hamilton of his recent conversion to Roman Catholicism, he was promptly asked by the Bishop to vacate his appointment as cathedral architect. Sir George Gilbert Scott was appointed after Henry Clutton's abrupt departure and was cathedral architect until his death in 1878.

Most of the grisaille window glass dates to the early 1860s and was made by Ward and Hughes, two of whose windows were removed in the 1960s and were destroyed before a public outcry saved the rest. The east window dates to 1982 and was made by the cathedral glazing department. At the foot of the north light is a panel portraying medieval farming scenes and the arms of the National Farmers Union who paid for the window on their 75th anniversary. The south panel portrays the insignia of the Armed Forces Nursing Services which surround the badge of the General Nursing Council.

The floor is of mid-19th century machine-made Minton tiles which replaced the earlier glorious 13th century hand-made encaustic tiles. The high water table prevented the construction of vaults beneath the floor. Part of these colourful medieval tiles may be discovered inserted into the floor of St Peter's chapel nearby *(see photograph on page 98)*.

Note the occasional (five) appearances of animals, birds, human and half-human figures which may be discovered, partly hidden, in the foliage at the top of the slender purbeck marble columns beside the stalls. The medieval family on the south wall is entrancing.

The chapter house also displays a wonderful selection of mostly original sculpted heads just below the frieze. It appears sculptors used a cross-section of local citizens as their models which, today, provide a homely view of the people living in Salisbury several hundred years ago. The two men with tongues out are said to represent 'blasphemy'.

The medieval three-faced sculpted head in the middle of the east wall is rare and of special significance. It may represent the qualities of circumspection (the president or chairman could not only see all that was going on; but also he was expected to discover what was in other people's minds – a leadership attribute greatly valued and respected in medieval times). Some believe it is a self-portrait of the master sculptor surveying his work. Other original medieval examples are in St. John Lateran in Rome, York chapter house (where the sculpture appears to be of a female) and in Llandaff cathedral.

The wooden table, which was extensively repaired in the 19th century, is said to have been around since the early days and may have been used for paying wages to the builders of the cathedral. A penny farthing a day seems to have been the usual wage.

The church plate in the exhibition cases has been brought in from parishes for safety or has been presented by benefactors. The silver is dated mostly to the 17th and 18th centuries. There are some very rare pieces of pre-Reformation silver (i.e. pre-1534) to be discovered in one of the cases. Note also the modern insignia of office, presented to the Clerk of Works by the Worshipful Company of Masons: also, the chalice used by the Rev George Herbert, Rector of Bemerton (1630-33) whose colourful memorial window is near the Gorges tomb in St Peter's chapel.

During warmer months there is a most interesting exhibition of medieval parchment books and other historical documents and objects on display in the chapter house. These may include Salisbury cathedral's beautifully illustrated Latin Gallican psalter (the book of the psalms) which dates to c. 970, a hundred years or so before the battle of Hastings, and has an interlinear translation into Anglo Saxon dating to about 1100. It is one of the earliest and best working examples in England and may have been in use by the royal Benedictine nunnery at Wilton where St Edith (the illegitimate daughter acknowledged by King Edgar, the first king of all England) flourished at about that time. Sometimes on display is the tiny document signed with a cross by the Lady Ela (widow of William Longespée, Earl of Salisbury) in 1240, professing her canonical obedience to Bishop Robert Bingham following her election as Abbess of Lacock Abbey. Parchment was animal skin usually taken from deer, cattle or sheep; though skin from goat, rabbit and squirrel was also used. The finest parchment was vellum, often made of calfskin or deerskin. The first supplies of paper came from the continent at the turn of the 13th century via the main English seaports.

There are fifty one stalls, i.e. seven groups of seven: plus two wide stalls at the western point of entry into the chapter house, which were reserved for the Chancellor and the Treasurer. History does not seem to relate who sat upon the fifty second seat!

In the restored tympanum (space), above the inside entry door of the chapter house, is a seated figure of Christ of the Apocalyptic Second Coming and the Book of Revelation. It is dated to about 1856 and is within a moulded frame in the corner of which are the symbols of Saints Matthew (man), Mark (lion), Luke (ox or calf) and John (eagle); see also Rev 4.7. The tympanum on the outside probably contained a medieval carving of the Coronation of the Virgin Mary as in the chapter house at York, but it was removed, probably at the Reformation.

As in the cathedral, the chapter house vault has little decoration and the eye is drawn upwards through the ribs and foliage to the roof. The vaulting bosses contain many more good human and animal representations; but, unfortunately, the majority cannot be seen clearly from ground level.

The iron and glass screen in the vestibule is 19th century: the painting on the vault is original and medieval.

Above the main entrance to the chapter house, between the door lintel and the surrounding arch, are fourteen voussoir (seen together, form an arch) carvings representing the virtues and vices. Although some restorations were made in the 19th century, the rest appear to be of mid 13th century origin. Note the virtues are all ladies who stand proudly with vanquished vices at their feet. There are explanatory notes and diagrams to be found nearby.

It is interesting to note that, according to Anderson's *History and Imagery in British Churches*, preaching friars in early medieval times were concerned with giving practical moral instruction rather than attempting to explain abstruse theology. Such lessons, if they were to be effective, had to be expressed dramatically. For example, the poem on the 'Psychomachia', written by Prudentius in the 4th century, described how the Virtues, in the shape of armed virgins, each engaged in single combat with the appropriate Vice and employed symbolic weapons. But some English artists from the 12th century onwards preferred to show the Virtues already triumphant and trampling on their foes. In Salisbury the Virtues are still noble ladies, as they were often described by their preachers, but the methods which they used to chastise their vanquished opponents have an element of grim comedy that foreshadows some of the later morality plays. Liberality is seen choking Avarice by ladling coins down his throat, Chastity is scourging Lust and Falsehood is having his tongue pulled out by Truth with an outsized pair of pincers. Other church designs elsewhere show Vice dangling from a miniature gallows; probably Doubt being despatched by Faith; for the suicide by hanging of Judas made this form of death a symbol of the ultimate sin – despair of God's forgiveness. However, Doubt's death by hanging is not shown in the Salisbury version.

Outside, the chapter house has grotesque waterspouts from each angle of the parapet.

Also displayed in the chapter house is one of four surviving original exemplifications of Magna Carta, sealed by King John and dated 15th June 1215 in the seventeenth year of his reign. A separate note on Magna Carta is at Chapter 3.

Dr Rodwell has noted 'that beautiful gem, the Salisbury sacristy, which is a miniature version of the chapter house, but has two storeys, is not widely known or appreciated and needs further study'. The sacristy is now the vestry (originally the treasury); its upper storey was once the muniment room where the chapter archives were kept. It is now the practice room for the choir, its glory is the 13th century handmade encaustic tiled floor in its original state (similar to the surviving part of the main floor in the Westminster Abbey chapter house), and is among the best examples in the country.

Salisbury Cathedral's Chapter House Frieze which was Completed c. 1266

The frieze comprises sixty delightful 13th century Old Testament vignettes carved in high relief on the spandrels of the arcading. There are fifty five scenes from the Book of Genesis and five scenes from the Book of Exodus, of these seven scenes depict the Creation; five of Adam and Eve; three of Cain and Abel, who are dressed as 13th century English peasants; four of Noah and the Flood; one of the Tower of Babel depicted as a medieval fortress; six of Lot and Abraham; eight of Jacob; twenty one of Joseph and five of Moses, ending with God presenting him with the tablets of stone on which the ten commandants were inscribed. They were originally painted and gilded offset by alternating blue and red grounds.

The frieze may well have been a practical reflection of the Fourth Lateran Council decisions of early 1215 presided over by Pope Innocent III and attended by Bishop Richard Poore (when he was Bishop of Chichester 1214-17) which, inter alia, called for the encouragement of improved religious education of those entering the church as a career.

The Salisbury frieze was damaged during the Commonwealth and Protectorate period 1649 - 1659; when the Puritans under Cromwell disbanded the Church of England and destroyed images of God, and some associated sculptures such as heads and limbs of men and beasts. This damage may have taken place in deference to the Parliamentary Commissioners who met in the chapter house.

The chapter house escaped the attentions of the architect James Wyatt in the late 18th century and gradually deteriorated. At the request of the Dean and Chapter in 1854, a full repair programme was directed by Henry Clutton, the architect, assisted by John Birnie Philip (the latter having shared responsibility with H M Armstead for designing the Royal Albert Memorial in Hyde Park) and his atelier were appointed to carry out remedial work on the frieze.

The artist Octavius Hudson was appointed by Philip to repaint the repaired sculptures and the surrounding walls. Unfortunately he did not prepare the surfaces properly and, by the end of the century, the paint had crumbled away and the Dean and Chapter ordered the remnants of the paint to be removed. Some of the 19th century paint may be discerned in the remains of roundels above the stalls.

Interesting research on the frieze by Dr. Pamela Z Blum, and others, suggest what is 13th century original and what is 19th century repair work or later.

Blum says that where the repairs have not disturbed, modified or distorted the original 13th century carving, it has been possible to distinguish the work of two entirely different medieval carvers. This has been achieved by comparing the figures e.g. the physical proportions, the style of the clothes, the composition of the picture, facial types and carving techniques. The carving of the first half of the frieze is generally better than the second half and quite different in detail. Both 13th century artists display their art of mime; the facial expressions are a delight to the viewer as are the physical gestures of arms and legs and the poses which reflect the mood and character of the unfolding stories. The people portrayed appear as seasoned actors and even groups of angels take up an amusing ballet stance. Note also that when God asked Cain 'Where is Abel, thy brother ?' Cain replied 'I know not. Am I my brother's keeper ?' A keen observer of the frieze will see Abel emerging from the ground below the tree on his way to heaven (*Gen IV, verses 8-11*).

Blum goes on to say that the first carver's ratio of head to body is 1:5 (his heads are larger, perhaps to cater for a view from below), whereas the second carver has a ratio of 1:6 or even 1:7 (the heads are smaller).The first man is good at story-telling using the minimum of space e.g. Noah enters the ark at one end and receives his dove at the other while the raven pecks away at a drowned horse in the background. His surviving heads are full of character e.g. Lot's family are very well presented and the dialogue between the drunken Noah and his sons is beautifully expressed. These heads represent high standards not achieved by the 19th century carvers. They are well worth a good look. The carving of Pharaoh and his Dream is entirely original and the vignette of Noah and the ark is complete, apart from the missing feet of the raven and the dove.

When Professor Sean McGrail, a distinguished expert on nautical shipping, examined the frieze in 1999 he noticed that Noah's ark had clinker laid (i.e. overlapping) planking of a type rarely seen; this is known as 'reverse-clinker' in which the higher plank laps inboard of the lower plank, rather than outboard as used in the Viking Age and the European clinker boats of today. McGrail suggests that the carver intended to represent medieval merchant ships known as hulcs or nordic post-Viking ships. Other medieval depictions of reverse-clinker planking have been found in 12th-14th century illuminated manuscripts and on the common seals of seaports. However it seems that, so far, no ship or boat of this construction has been excavated in Europe.

As with a study of the 13th century original carvings, a study of the 19th century repairs indicates the presence of two, possibly three, carvers and occasionally a surprising lack of daily supervision of their work. The main difference being that the original carving was carried out on Chilmark stone, whereas the 19th century additions are mainly on Caen stone or pierre factice (manufactured stone) which, today, is mostly of a lighter or much darker colour.

Examples of unsupervised rough work by the 19th century carvers on the sixth day of the Creation include the replacement of the horse (upper left of the carving) with the body of a cow; but retaining the horse's flowing tail. Note also that the damaged sheep below has a pig's head and a pig's forelegs. According to ancient drawings a sheep has been added where there was none in the original picture. The delicate balance of the original medieval design in this vignette, says Dr Blum, is thus rather cluttered.

Dean Ralph Brideoake's Prayer Desk

This fine wooden desk was carved by Alexander Fort in 1672 for Ralph Brideoake, the Dean of Salisbury 1667 – 1675, and was placed at the SW end of Salisbury Cathedral's choir. It is now in the Cathedral's Morning Chapel and is remarkable for its delightful rebuses (SOED part definition – rebus from the Latin suggesting a device, often of heraldic appearance, indicating the name of the bearer).

Dean Ralph Brideoake's Prayer Desk
carved by Alexander Fort 1672.

One rebus is illustrated by two clasped hands suggesting the Dean's happy marriage and also the first part of the Dean's surname. Another rebus is its beautifully carved large English oak tree which celebrates not only the second half of the Dean's surname but was most probably a reflection of the country's joy at King Charles' escape from pursuing Parliamentarians in 1651, following the disastrous battle of Worcester, by hiding in the branches of the famous Boscobel oak. This brilliant escapade, together with the restoration of the monarchy and the Church of England in 1660 was, at that time, still very much in people's minds.

Congratulations to readers who may find another possible rebus in the carving of this desk concerning his happy marriage.

Green Men

In lighter vein, and to answer questions from the reader, it may be of interest to indicate why there are so many Green Men around the cathedral. According to *Brewer's Dictionary of Phrase and Fable*, the origin of the Green Man seems to have been a cultural symbol (around much of the world) of created fertility in nature. In Christian terms he is the symbol of Easter and the Resurrection and is usually depicted as a gentle and humble deity.

Mary McGill, Blue Badge Guide, has noted that the faces of Green Men are magical imaginings of medieval man. Mary goes on to say 'we have no idea of what they meant to their creators and, since the Reformation, their original significance seems to have disappeared into the past. Oak leaves spring out of their mouths, nostrils and ears. They have staring eyes. Leaves spread out and become garlands round their heads. There are winding branches of hawthorn and honeysuckle round their necks.

Some are simpler than others, some more frightening and some are welcoming. The hawthorn wards off evil. The oaks were the mainstay of the common people's lives for wood was used in their houses, boats, ships and weapons. They worshipped plants so important in their daily lives. Leaves were also symbols of lust and desires of the flesh, they may also represent death in winter, rebirth in Spring. People respected nature which was all powerful.

The earliest of the Green Men probably appeared in the late 4th or 5th centuries and, when introduced, were automatically baptised – they were not ugly or distorted but were much loved. Later it became almost impossible to enter a medieval church in England and not find a Green Man – they became very popular and a guardian symbol over doorways, entrances and pillars and were easily assimilated into our pre-Christian past.

The skills of simple people would have been handed down from father to son and absorbed by those around them. Their creators would have passed the long winter evenings listening to stories from the past and so combined the past with the present in the sculptures they created. Every Green Man would have been different, reflecting the thoughts, ideas and faith of the man who chiselled their faces and placed them in our medieval churches.

The Heads of St John the Baptist

The Chilmark stone (sandy limestone) statue of St John the Baptist appears standing high up on the west face of the south central buttress of Salisbury Cathedral's west front. Since c. 1340 he has had a good view through the Close, over the Avon River and across Salisbury's ancient water meadows. By c. 1851, a pencil drawing by C.R. Cockerell clearly shows John holding a clypeus (a round shield) depicting the Agnus Dei (Lamb of God). But, sadly, it also shows that John had weathered badly and had lost his head again.

Readers may recall that John originally lost his head after he had reminded King Herod that it was against the law for him to marry a lady called Herodias because she was the King's sister-in-law. When Herodias was told of this she was hopping mad and was determined to get her own back on John. Her chance came during Herod's birthday party at which her daughter, Salome, performed before Herod the dance of the seven veils. Herod, overcome with delight and desire, whispered to Salome "Ask me anything you like and I will give it to you, even half my kingdom". Thereupon, Salome glided out and asked her mother "What shall I reply?" Herodias replied at once "Tell him to give me John the Baptist's head" she cried. "here and now, on a dish". Salome ran back to King Herod and delivered the message. Deeply distressed, Herod ordered his bodyguard to bring the head and then presented it to Salome's mother.

Many centuries later a certain gentleman, while ambling through Salisbury Cathedral's Close – somewhat the worst for wear – noticed a ladder placed against the west front wall of the cathedral. Full of curiosity he climbed the ladder unsteadily and found himself, red-face to bearded-face, with St John the Baptist. After greeting him affectionately, he patted his cheek and the head fell into his arms. He could find nowhere to put it; so he tucked it under his arm and descended gingerly down the ladder. Then, discovering a sack nearby, put the head inside, slung it over his shoulder and off he went. But a security guard approached him and asked to look inside the sack.

It seems that the authorities dealt with him leniently and John the Baptist's head was soon replaced. And that was how St John the Baptist lost his head a third time.

An Ancient Description of Salisbury Cathedral

The following was quoted by Daniel Defoe (author of Robinson Crusoe) in his 'Journey through England' in about 1722.

> *"As many days as in one year therebe,*
> *So many windows in one church we see;*
> *As many marble pillars there appear,*
> *As there are hours throughout the fleeting year:*
> *As many gates as moons one year do view:*
> *Strange tale to tell, yet not more strange than true".*

Clockwork

Salisbury medieval clock, which is made of hand-wrought iron c. 1386, is probably the oldest working clock in Europe. It was originally housed in the Bell Tower on the open ground just north of the cathedral. The tower was pulled down in 1792 and the clock was moved to the cathedral tower where it worked until it was replaced in 1884. In 1956 it was taken out of retirement and repaired by antiquarian horologists and set up in its present position. It never had a face and the passage of time was indicated by the striking of a bell situated in the triforium above.

At present the clock is regularly serviced by Mr Mike Bell who is an experienced horologist and a master of his trade. On a recent visit to the Cathedral Mike notes that the clock was made to run for 12 hours – dawn to dusk – the ecclesiastical hours.

There would be 12 turns of rope around the barrel of the Going Train. The weights broke the day into 12 parts – in the summer they would have to fit 12 'hours' into a 16 hour day. In the winter 12 'hours' into an 8 hour day.

Mr Bell adds that Cistercians were able to have only two daily meals in the winter, because that would be all the time available for them to get through 12 prayer sessions in 8 hours! e.g. 40 minute gaps in the winter and 1 hour 20 minutes in the summer.

The weights were moved in or out to speed or slow the timing; the further in the faster the wheel would go, and further out the slower it would go. In fact medieval clocks were like mechanical computers working out the days. Screws weren't invented until 1540, hence it looks as if the clock had been designed by a carpenter!

The clockmakers would have been highly educated. It is believed that the Cathedral's medieval clock was made by Johannes and Williemus Vrieman and Johannes Jietuijt of Delft. They would probably have spoken Dutch, Latin, Norman French and Chaucer's English.

Appendix I

The Knights Templar and the Knights of St John of Jerusalem

1. The Knights Templar were Founded c. 1118 and Suppressed by Pope Clement V on 22 March 1312

The Templars were a religious and military organisation of soldier monks founded in 1118 by Hugh of Payens (from Champagne in France) in Jerusalem to protect the Holy Sepulchre and to provide safety and welfare for pilgrims visiting the Holy Land. Hugh and his companions persuaded Baldwin I, King of Jerusalem, to set apart an area of the royal palace – once the Mosque of Al Aqsa – where his group which, initially, were obedient to the Benedictines, could carry out increased charitable work and recruit more members. The group expanded rapidly and soon declared themselves an independent Order devoted, not just to protecting pilgrims, but to the creation of an establishment of military knights bound by religious vows of personal poverty; chastity and obedience, which owed allegiance to the Pope in Rome; and devoted themselves to fighting against marauding heathens. Thus the Knights Templar came into being.

The Order was divided into three classes. Knights, all of noble birth, whose badge was the red cross, worn on a white tunic; sergeants at-arms and sergeants, drawn from the bourgeoisie, who wore their red cross on a black tunic; and clerics who were in charge of non-military charitable tasks. The first duty of the Order was to keep the road from the Mediterranean coast to Jerusalem free from marauders. But, as their numbers increased, they began to take part, alongside the Hospitallers, in major military campaigns. Hugh, now Grand Master of the Order, spent much of his subsequent time in Western Europe recruiting for his Order at which he was overwhelmingly successful.

St Bernard, Abbott of Clairvaux, became their patron. Popes and Kings gave valuable support in the form of cash, gifts of land and the award of valuable privileges to individuals. Temples and churches were built in many European cities to a circular design resembling the domed building raised over the site of the Holy Sepulchre where Jesus was laid. In England, King Henry II became such a strong supporter of the Temple in London (completed in 1185 and consecrated by Heraclius, Patriarch of Jerusalem) that he declared publicly his wish to be buried there. So, accordingly, the church was enlarged to cater for his wishes. But he seems to have changed his mind, for when he died in 1189 he was buried in Fontevrault, Marne, France.

The Knights Templar, together with the Hospitallers, provided reliable military support for the Crusaders. But, eventually, the Templars became very rich (they were bankers for the Crusades), over-powerful and arrogant. After the fall of Acre in 1291 they became extremely unpopular with European royalty, the Pope in Rome and the people. Complaints were lodged; allegations of 'heresy' and 'evil practices' were made. Courts of investigation were set up. Many confessions of guilt were obtained sometimes, it was said, by torture and unexplained 'other means'. The Knights Templar's Order was suppressed by Pope Clement V on 22 March 1312.

In England the Order had its first house (c. 1121) near Holborn Bars, London; and moved to its present site off Fleet Street (c. 1160). This Temple Church, with its circular design, was severely bombed during the Second World War on 10 May 1941. It was repaired and renovated and is now situated in a particularly peaceful and beautiful part of London. It is the spiritual home of the legal profession whose practices are in the Inner and Middle

Temple and is an interesting and lively place of public worship (Church of England). The Temple Church contains effigies of former Templars, including William The Marshal, first Earl of Pembroke (2nd creation) and quondam Regent of England during Henry III's minority (died 1219) which, though painstakingly repaired, are extremely well carved. Other interesting effigies are in the cast court of the V & A Museum, London. There is also some excellent stained glass to admire and, for those who are curious, more than a hint of the 'Da Vinci Code' to discover in the Temple Church ....

The Knights of St John of Jerusalem (the Hospitallers) were Founded c. 1020 and have Survived as a most Successful International Non-Militant Charitable Organisation into the 21st Century

King Richard The Lionheart Knight of the Hospitallers of Jerusalem.

When the victorious Crusaders entered Jerusalem in 1099, they discovered a hospice (a place of care) run by members and merchants from Amalfi, and other pious citizens, since c. 1020. They were obedient to a nearby Benedictine Abbey and had dedicated themselves to St John the Almoner, a seventh century Cypriot, who became Patriarch of Antioch. Their avowed task included provision for the safe lodging of visitors to the Holy Land. By 1090 the Hospital was run by Fra Gerardo Sasso da Scala who invited knights and other pilgrims to help him expand his good work. Thus was born a separate new Order of St John of Jerusalem, also known as the Order of the Knights Hospitallers, which soon became obedient to the Pope in Rome. In 1113 it was formally incorporated by a bull (from medieval Latin for a round object, such as the seal of lead attached to a papal edict) issued by Pope Pascall II. A little later St John the Baptist was substituted for the lesser known St John the Almoner. The distinctive badge of the Hospitallers was a white cross of eight points (signifying the eight Beatitudes) on a black ground which they wore on their tunics over armour. A commanderie or branch was established in England c. 1148 at Clerkenwell where their church, much rebuilt, still stands.

The main aim of the Order was the relief of suffering (as it is today). Members took solemn vows of poverty, chastity and obedience. In earliest days the military protection of pilgrims to the Holy Land was the task of the Templars. But, when serious fighting between Saracen-led marauders and Christian settlers broke out, the Knights Hospitallers adopted a military role as their second activity. They built a number of substantial castles such as the Crac de Chevaliers. Soon the Hospitallers and the Templars formed the equivalent of a major regular army of well-trained, well-equipped (with armour, sword and horse) and highly-

The Blessed Raymond du Puy de Provence, French Knight of the Hospitallers of Jerusalem, painted by Alexandre Laenlein.
He established military protection for foreign visitors to the Holy places in Jerusalem and became, for many years, the Second Grand Master of the Order of St John.

Crac des Cavaliers, Medieval Crusader castle of the Hospitallers of Jerusalem.

motivated soldiers engaged in a Holy War. They achieved much fame as the result of their knowledge of the countryside, their relationships with, and understanding of, a wide variety of people, their customs, their languages and their local politics. On the other hand, many Crusaders tended to be visitors in a strange country, often on the outlook for loot and treasure, and soon to long for a return (victorious and rich or disheartened and defeated) to their countries of origin. The Hospitallers retained the respect of the population by continuing the distribution of alms to the poor of Jerusalem, and other charitable activities, with a generosity which astonished foreign visitors.

In 1187, after the battle of Hattin, Saladin and the Saracens recaptured Jerusalem compelling the Hospitallers and the Templars to restrict their activities to the coastline of Palestine and to limited forays inland. When the town of Acre fell to militant Islam in 1291 (both the Marshal of the Order and the Master were killed) despite the bravery of the Templars and the Hospitallers, the Hospitallers fell back to Kolossi in Cyprus in 1301. They took over the defence of Rhodes and its islands in 1310 and were styled the Knights of Rhodes; but were driven out by the Ottomans. In 1530 they were given Malta as their base and stayed there for two centuries defending the islands throughout the Great Siege from the Ottomans. Grand Master La Valletta gave his name to the capital city and built the extensive fortifications which exist today. While in Malta the Order ran a health service for the Maltese people and set up a famous school of anatomy and surgery. The great ward in Malta's hospital was the longest room in 18th century Europe. Their magnificent defence of Malta in 1565 enabled unhindered passage of Christian shipping through the Mediterranean; and they took part in the defeat of the Muslim armada at the battle of Lepanto in 1571.

This signalled the decline of Muslim sea power in the Mediterranean. Eventually the Hospitallers last Grand Master surrendered to the powerful armies of Napoleon Bonaparte in 1798.

Having been expelled from Malta the Sovereign Order of Malta and the Knights of Malta, as they had become, found refuge in Rome in 1834 where they abandoned their military role and reverted to charitable work among the sick and poor.

In Britain, following the establishment of a commanderie at Clerkenwell in the mid 13th century, the activities of the Order expanded rapidly as new commanderies were formed. Eventually Clerkenwell became a priory with a number of commanderies; and other priories with their commanderies were established across England, Scotland and Wales. Ireland had its own separate priory.

In 1540 the Order came to an end in England during the Reformation and the Dissolution of the Monasteries, when King Henry VIII proclaimed himself Protector of the Order; and then arranged for the Order to be sequestrated, and its property handed over to the

Crown. The Order was restored by Queen Mary in 1557 only to be suppressed again by Queen Elizabeth I. Whereupon the Order fell into abeyance.

During the industrial revolution in Britain in the 19th century a number of charitable organisations were formed to alleviate the sufferings of the poor. Among these was The St John Ambulance Brigade which originated in 1873 to provide first aid and care to the public and became a Foundation in 1887. The St John Ambulance Association, which provided first aid training to the public, was established in 1877; and the St John of Jerusalem Eye Hospital Foundation which was established in Palestine in 1882 *(see below)*.

Meanwhile these organisations became very popular and were supported by a sympathetic public which included many well-known royal personages. In 1888 Queen Victoria presented St John Ambulance Association with a new Charter which re-united all these organisations to form The Order of St John. This new Order was the first and only provider of a trained ambulance service, including nurses, to look after the sick and injured in hospitals and in their homes until the formation of the National Health Service in 1946.

In 1961 a convention of alliance with the Orders of St John in Germany, the Netherlands and Sweden was formed. Close relations were also instituted with the Sovereign Order in Rome. It flourishes today in many countries abroad and within the Commonwealth.

There was a major reconstruction of the English Order's constitution in 1999. This resulted in the formation of a Grand Council, the removal of restrictions as to nationality and religious belief for membership of the Order; and established a new Priory to carry out its activities in England.

Today The St John of Jerusalem Eye Hospital in Palestine is a Foundation of the Order of St John and claims to be the oldest registered charity in the world. It is the main provider of eye care in the West Bank, Gaza and East Jerusalem. In 2008 it treated 94,426 patients of whom 25,579 were under the age of 18. The Hospital also trains doctors and nurses especially from among the local population. Patients are treated regardless of race, religion or ability to pay.

Appendix II

The College of De Vaux in Salisbury and its Neighbour St Nicholas Hospital.

De Vaux College was Founded by Bishop Giles de Bridport in 1260 and Dissolved in 1543, for Religious and Political Reasons, during the Reformation

During the last 150 years or so historians generally assumed that the College of De Vaux was the first residential university college, with a settled government, in England. But the historian, Professor Nicholas Orme of Exeter University, has recently concluded

'In the educational league-table of medieval England, Salisbury and its cathedral were in the first division – but not the premier league. Salisbury was not like Oxford, Cambridge, or London, with huge numbers of students and very advanced kinds of study. Rather, it was one of a dozen or so important provincial centres of education, like Bristol, Canterbury, Exeter, Lincoln, Norwich, Wells and York'.

Nicholas Orme continues
'De Vaux is interesting as an early attempt to provide support for the scholars of such a city and as the only one to help them study theology as well as grammar. But it was never copied elsewhere. For most of the time the cathedral's involvement with children and education was routine and unobtrusive. We cannot trace the cathedral's effects on young people and there is scarcely a famous person who can be said to have gone to its schools, but that does not mean that the cathedral authorities did not do valuable work in this field. It trained choristers and altarists, ran a grammar school in addition to De Vaux College, and provided lectures for clergy. It sent out several thousand pupils …. with greater or lesser skills, and shaped their lives. The likelihood is that there were many people, clergy and laity, who were grateful for that'.

Old Sarum itself was regarded as a safe haven for fugitive students who were compelled to flee from Oxford to continue their studies temporally in peaceful academic surroundings. For example in 1209 Oxford students accidentally killed a woman and the Oxford townspeople reacted by hanging three students. The church authorities laid an interdict over Oxford and three thousand students fled into the countryside. In 1238, shortly after Cardinal Otho, the Legate of Pope Gregorious IX, came to England, a poor half-starved Irish Chaplain came to the door of the Legate's kitchen at Osney Abbey asking for food. The Master of the Cooks, who was the Legate's brother, threw

De Vaux College c. early 19th century. St Nicholas Road, Salisbury.

some hot greasy water into his face. Nearby students fell on the Master and killed him (poor Cardinal Otho, locked himself up in a church tower and at night fled for his life). Oxford was laid under another interdict this time 'by bell, book and candle' and once more the students fled. Some came to Salisbury where, for a time, they would have continued their education under the Cathedral Chancellor.

Bishop Giles (or Aedigius) de Bridport was born in the late 12th century, or early in the 13th century, and was Bishop of Salisbury from 1256 to 1262. Like some public figures today with their many directorships, Giles was a pluralist and held many offices in the gift of Pope and King (Henry III). He became comparatively rich but he was not regarded as a greedy man. Indeed when he took over the bishopric he found the cathedral almost built, but without a roof. It seems that, at his own expense, he generously covered the roof in lead. He had considerable expertise in both legal and spiritual matters and represented his monarch in negotiations with the Pope. He presided over the hallowing of the cathedral by Archbishop Boniface on 20 September 1258 in the presence of King Henry III and Queen Eleanor. Bishop Giles died on 13 September 1262 and his beautiful tomb is on the south side of the south choir aisle. His 19th century statue may be seen among the lowest row of ecclesiastical worthies on the west front of Salisbury Cathedral.

In February 1260 the Dean and Chapter gave Bishop Giles the Wardenship of St.Nicholas's Hospital and, in the same year, he founded the College of De Vaux in a vacant area opposite the Hospital. The College's foundation charter, which is still in the cathedral library, includes the following statement 'to the honour of the Lord Jesus and the Glorious Virgin Mary and Blessed Nicholas, for the salvation of our soul, and for the souls of our benefactors, and of all those to whom we are bound…(I have)…thought fit to found, establish and build a house for the use and ownership of scholars which shall forever be called 'the house of the Valley Scholars of the Blessed St.Nicholas'…in a meadow near the Cathedral church of Salisbury and the King's Way in front of the (Blessed Nicholas) Hospital, for the perpetual reception and maintenance of a Warden for the time being, two chaplains and twenty poor needy honest and docile scholars serving God and the Blessed Nicholas…studying and becoming proficient in the Holy Scriptures and the liberal arts…free to enjoy for ever…all exactions and taxes…and free from all secular service and demand'.

As will be seen later the seeds of the College's eventual destruction were sown in the first paragraph of the quotation above.

By early 1263, seven weeks after the death of Bishop Giles, the College had amassed quite considerable endowments in Berkshire, Dorsetshire and Wiltshire including eighteen librates of rent in the City of Sarum (a librate is a pound's worth of land). Five hides of land in Lavington Episcopi, Washing, Hertlye and Brewerfield (a hide is the area of family land ranging from sixty to a hundred and twenty acres). Six acres of land in Dewlish, Alyngton (a suburb of Bridport) and Walditch. The advowsons of the churches at Milborne St. Andrew, Alyngton and Walditch (an advowson was the guardianship or patronage of an ecclesiastical house or benefice. Nowadays it is the right of presentation to a benefice OED); and all the buildings of the College itself.

Sir John Holteby, a Canon of the Cathedral, was appointed first resident Warden of the College. Thus De Vaux College was well-found and soon began to play an important part in the education of young men destined to make their careers in local churches. De Vaux College scholars were compelled to celebrate annually the commemoration of their founder in the parish church of Bridport (Bishop Giles' probable birthplace). During the two hundred and eighty years of its existence the College developed a somewhat tenuous connection with Oxford University i.e. one or two students a year might have been accepted by that university.

In addition to the limited space in the College, scholars may have been taught in the nave of the cathedral, in the transepts or in the cloisters. For the last hundred years of the College's existence some of the scholars may have been taught in part of the New Library (after 1445) which was demolished in 1776.

There were no printed books available in the early days. Everything had to be written or copied by hand on vellum (animal skin), manuscripts were costly and few in number, oral instruction was by means of lectures, conversations and disputations. According to 'the Religious Houses of Wiltshire', only 114 names of fellows and chaplains educated at De Vaux College during the 280 years of its existence have been traced. Most of the students came from the local population and it is interesting to note that a greater proportion of lawyers to theologians graduated from the College which was founded originally for the liberal arts and theology. This tendency annoyed the Dean and Chapter and in 1473 William Ashley, a College fellow, was told that having obtained his MA degree he should proceed to the study of theology and on no account to civil law. Very little is known of the social origin of the De Vaux scholars, though it is known that William Harding (a fellow in 1470) was the bastard son of Master William Harding BCL himself a former fellow of De Vaux, who served as Chapter Clerk of Salisbury Cathedral for about thirty years.

De Vaux scholars were required by their Charter to be poor; but generous benefactors helped. In 1267 Robert Careville (the Cathedral Treasurer) left each scholar half a mark for the purchase of a habit; he left to the house itself all his working utensils and his spoons. In 1490 Thomas de Boyton left a quarter of his estate to the Vaux scholars who were studying at Oxford (unfortunately, no numbers or names were given).

Nicholas Upton, Warden of the College, and Simon Hutchings, a fellow of the College, were the two proctors who were sent to Rome in 1456 as representatives of the Bishop, Dean and Chapter of Salisbury Cathedral in connection with the long-delayed canonisation of Bishop Osmund (who died in 1099). They succeeded where so many others had failed. Hutchings was a generous benefactor of the College and is known to have carried out a full repair of the college buildings as well as refurbishing the chapel and doing 'many other good things'.

Although De Vaux College was not part of a monastery it was founded as an institution for celebates. Therefore, how remarkable it was that, on the 14th May 1317, a deed was signed by which the Warden and scholars unanimously and willingly granted to Roger Moton and his wife Christina (who had been considerable benefactors of the College) the partaking of food in the house until they died. The former was to sit next to Roger Fouk for as long as Roger Fouk lived and thereafter to take his place. Christina on the other hand could sit where she liked and could have a chamber built for her at her husband's expense. Roger Moton was allowed to build a stable for one horse. Roger and Christina could come and go as if they were scholars.

George Sydenham (Archdeacon of the Cathedral whose cadaver monument is in the north choir aisle) was one of the last Wardens of De Vaux College and held the post from 1507 till his death in 1524. He had been Chaplain to Kings Henry VII and Henry VIII.

Sydenham's successor as Warden was Thomas Martin, a Residentiary Canon of the Cathedral. He lived for little more than a year in the appointment and on his death no one seemed keen to take his place. Times were hard for the English clergy. It was no secret that small religious institutions were in danger of suppression by King Henry VIII in his need to raise money and that their endowments might be confiscated by him at any time. Be this as it may, on 3rd March 1526, in the presence of the Vale scholars, the Dean and Chapter declared that the scholars should remove themselves to Oxford or somewhere else. None were to remain in Salisbury after the ninth day of the following month excepting the two stewards, two chaplains, the cook and the butler under pain of losing their scholarships. Not all the scholars approved this drastic action and some declined to leave. Domini John Chapman, Hermey and one of the chaplains were summoned to appear before the Dean and Chapter on 27th April 1526. They were pronounced contumascious and in contempt and were deprived of their commons until they should leave to study at Oxford.

The depleted College continued in existence for seventeen more years although in greatly reduced circumstances. In 1543 (John Biggs was the last Warden) the College was dissolved formally and pensions were paid to two chaplains and eight fellows or scholars. The endowment of the College in 1535 included property in Dorsetshire, Berkshire, Wiltshire and in New Sarum. The total annual income at that time was £94. 15s. 0 ½d.

The College failed not for educational reasons; but because many of its endowed properties and possessions had been given with the proviso that prayers should be offered in perpetuity for the souls of benefactors. And so it shared the fate of other chantry chapels which fell under King Henry VIII's Chantries Act. This Act assigned to the Crown all chantries, colleges and hospitals which offered prayers for people's souls in return for money or gifts received. Land confiscated by the Crown was almost immediately sold. The historian Camden estimated that a total of 2374 chantries and chapels, 90 colleges and 110 hospitals were involved. Thus the day to day lives of people were more affected by this action than by the dissolution of the monasteries which had taken place earlier. It was all part of the Act of Supremacy (1534) and the Protestant Reformation in England. It is clear that the action taken by the Dean and Chapter was timely and achieved without financial loss to the cathedral authorities. The actual site of the college and other small endowments were either sold or granted to various citizens in and around Salisbury.

It seems as if the buildings of De Vaux College continued to disintegrate over the years. William Naish's map of Salisbury dated 1751, some two hundred years after the College was suppressed, shows the outline of the College as an inverted letter L to the west of St Nicholas's Hospital. In Benson's delineation of 1820 entitled 'the Remains of the College De Vaux from the South' shows a two-storied stone building looking rather like some of the existing older buildings in St Nicholas's Hospital opposite. See illustration on *p.114*.

According to the Sarum Architects' Partnership, whose practice, at one time, was based in De Vaux House, the buildings of De Vaux College formed a rectangular block which was the usual medieval pattern. From the corner where St Nicholas Road and De Vaux Place meet, its longer side stretched westward towards the Harnham Gate at the south end of the Close. Its shorter side extended southwards towards the River Avon. Hidden away from public view was a courtyard giving access to the College rooms. The coat of arms presently attached to the east wall is that of Oxford University and is of modern construction.

A subsequent fire split the ancient remains of De Vaux College into two which are now known as De Vaux Lodge to the south and De Vaux House to the north. The Royal Commission on Historic Monuments states that the walls and roof of De Vaux Lodge include medieval material from the College; but the medieval windows shown in an engraving of 1834 are no longer to be seen (Note: they must have been replaced earlier in the 19th century). An ashlar quoin at the north east corner is probably medieval and the roof includes stout smoke-blackened rafters with mortices in positions which suggest a former scissor-braced rafter roof probably of the 13th century. De Vaux House, the Royal Commissioners state, is mainly of the 17th century but it incorporates walls which probably come from a building associated with the College. A plan of c. 1825 names this site 'Magdalen Penitentiary'.

Myrfield House to the north of De Vaux House was built in 1812 on the site of an older building shown on Naish's map of 1751. The north side of the garden is bounded by the Cathedral Close wall built of stones brought down from the cathedral in Old Sarum by licence of King Edward III in 1332/3. The original masons' marks on these stones, dated to the late 11th century, may still be clearly seen. The range of single-storied buildings to the east and west of Myrfield House are of the 17th or 18th century and were originally cottages and shops. Along the south side of De Vaux Place is a terrace of six houses, each of three storeys, built c. 1826 by John Peniston (1778-1840), the county surveyor.

This stone came from the Chilmark quarries c. 1100 and was used to build the original castle or Cathedral on top of Old Sarum Hill. In c. 1333 it would have been brought down to Salisbury to construct the great wall which surrounds most of the Cathedral Close.
The Mason's mark (probably incised to indicate daily progress of his manual work) is clearly seen.

Some members of the Sarum Architects' Partnership are amongst those who claim that De Vaux House is haunted. Apparently there were several sightings of a grey shadowy figure of a woman. Once her head and body were seen leaning out of a window at a time when the positioning of the furniture would have made this physically impossible. She has also appeared in other rooms. Perhaps this is the ghost of Christina Moton looking for an agreeable companion with whom to share her commons at table.

St Nicholas Hospital (the Hostelry at the Ford on the banks of the River Avon)

The earliest surviving record of St Nicholas Hospital dates from 1215, five years before the foundation stones of Salisbury Cathedral were laid, when Richard Aucher signed a document by which he gave 10 acres of land in "Fissherton" to "God and the Hospital of St Nicholas at (Salisbury) for the Master and Brethren who serve God in that place".

In 1227 Ela, Countess of Salisbury and widow of William Longspée Earl of Salisbury endowed the Hospital with some 60 head of cattle, 12 horses, 60 pigs and 300 sheep. Also in the same year, Bishop Richard le Poore (Bishop of Salisbury 1217 – 28), 'having considered the inadequate resources of the Hospital, arranged an endowment for the maintenance of a chaplain to celebrate divine things in the Hospital chapel... and for the comfort of poor persons, and travellers crossing the river or turning aside to rest there'.

The Hospital was dedicated to St Nicholas who was the local patron saint of travellers. The word Hospital comes from the same source as the word hotel and was used in this instance to describe an inn, guesthouse or hostel which offered hospitality to those in need such, as travellers who had crossed the River Avon by a nearby ford, and who required to rest before travelling to or from Old Sarum. The ford was part of the main road from Sarum to the south coast.

In 1229 Bishop Bingham (Bishop of Salisbury 1229 – 47) who was busily engaged with the building of the new Cathedral took a special interest in St Nicholas Hospital. He built a stone bridge in two parts over the divided river (note the recently inscribed stone on the western side of the bridge). "It is built of stone", he said "to last, if God so grants, for all time". He built a Chapel on the island between the two rivers and dedicated it to St John the Baptist (this island is still known locally as St John's Island and the Chapel can still be traced in the house there now known as 'St. John's Isle'). Such bridge-chapels were a common feature in medieval times. In pre-Christian times they were thought of as a defence against the Spirit of the River which might try to sweep away the bridge; but later they came to be regarded as holy places where travellers might give thanks to God for a safe crossing.

Bishop Bingham appears also to have built many new buildings and drew up rules of life for its staff. In addition to being responsible for the Hospital, the Master of the Hospital was also required to look after the bridge and to service its chapel. The building of the bridge changed the main objects of the Hospital from looking after travellers to caring for the poor, sick and elderly. It is interesting to note that, in Bishop Bingham's Ordinance, Sisters are mentioned for the first time as among those 'who serve God in this place'.

In Bishop Beauchamp's time (1450 – 82) life in St Nicholas Hospital had become the source of some public concern; matters had to be rectified by a new set of rules. The Bishop ordained 'if any brother or sister be a frequent stirrer of strife, he must be expelled'. Furthermore, 'brothers and sisters must not behave in a suspicious manner, either in their own rooms or in hidden places, nor must they live together in one room, unless they have been lawfully married before admission', and, 'begging expeditions through the neighbouring villages must stop'. The Master was instructed to see that the brethren were provided with enough money to buy clothing, wood, coal, food and the services of a barber and a washerwoman. Thus the rules of the Hospital were changed again. The Bishop also reconstructed the Hospital and converted one of its two chapels to secular use.

There was a vital difference between the original charter, as amended, of St Nicholas Hospital and that of the College of the De Vaux scholars. The former was founded mainly for the relief of travellers and later for the comfort of the poor and needy. The College of De Vaux was founded mainly for the salvation of Bishop Giles de Bridport's soul and for the souls of various other worthies – thus the college was to all intents and purposes a chantry and the seeds of its eventual destruction were there from the very beginning. For it was Henry VIII's abolition of chantry chapels and confiscation of their endowments that sealed the fate of the College of De Vaux following the establishment of a catholic but reformed Church of England (in fact the Dean and Chapter of Salisbury Cathedral appear to have beaten the gun in 1536 and they themselves abolished the college at no loss to themselves).

Thus St Nicholas Hospital escaped the effects of the abolition of chantry chapels although the Bridge Chapel itself was suppressed at that time. In 1550 Henry Herbert, soon to succeed his father as the Earl of Pembroke, was made Master: It was hoped that his local influence in difficult times would enable the Hospital to survive. In 1610 King James I issued Letters Patent laying down the rules which would govern the affairs of the Hospital and they remained in force until 1959. During the Commonwealth period (1649 – 60) the Master, together with the Bishop and clergy of the Cathedral, fled abroad and the Mayor and City Council took over the control of the Cathedral, the Close and the Hospital. All returned with the Restoration and life continued much as before.

In the mid-1850s Anthony Trollope published his novel 'The Warden' describing the life and activities of the Master of St Nicholas Hospital (aka Hiram's Hospital). It soon became a world classic exposing the existence of smug sinecures in the Church 'an egregious malversation of charity', he said, and called for reform.

Since 1959 the Hospital has been governed by its own Act of Parliament and a fresh Board of Trustees reorganised the finances and the administration. Over succeeding years they have carried out major new building programmes and a modernisation of the accommodation.

Parts of the original 13th century buildings may still be recognised. It seems that St Nicholas Hospital was rather different from others built at the same time. Instead of the usual long building with a chapel at the east end together with another long building with cells each opening into a hall from either side to form a common dining room, St Nicholas Hospital had two chapels separated by an arcade down the whole length of the building, half of the building was for the men and the other half was for the women. One of the chapels was dedicated to St Nicholas and the other to St Mary the Virgin.

Among the items of historical interest which have survived are the 14th century tiles in the sanctuary, the 1623 chapel bell, the 17th century oak table, the 18th century pewter plates and the Act of Parliament clock which is dated 1760.

Appendix III

The Yankalilla Connection

By 1887 Salisbury Cathedral's 17th century Restoration font had been retired to a garden within the Cathedral Close. One day a passing clergyman (the Rev C Morse, Vicar of Christ Church, Yankalilla, Australia) while on holiday in England, was strolling through the Close when he noticed the font and he reflected how appropriate it would look in his little church in the Australian outback. So, plucking up courage, he asked the Cathedral authorities if he might have it. After investigation the Dean and Chapter decided that the font might be more usefully employed in the vicar's church at Yankalilla. And so it came to pass that Salisbury's redundant font was safely installed in Christ Church Yankalilla some eighty kilometres SW of Adelaide.

Christ Church, Yankalilla, built 1852. Inside there is a Marian Shrine and the resting place of Salisbury Cathedral's 17th century font. It is 80 kilometers SW of Adelaide, Australia.

Yankalilla was the original home of Australian aborigines. A rough translation of its name is 'the Place by the Stream'. Sadly there are no aborigines left in the area but their presence in the past may be discovered in local place names, and on ancient tree trunks from which large patches of bark have been cut for use by Aborigines in the construction of their little river boats.

A few years ago, following a whitewash of the church, a strange apparition of the Virgin Mary appeared on a wall. This caused a sensation resulting in worldwide interest whereupon the Diocesan Bishop declared the church to be a Marian shrine.

Author's Note:
Unfortunately, when I visited the church in 2000, the apparition had all but disappeared. However the constant stream of visitors from the rest of Australia and abroad has continued unabated and produces a very respectable income too. Whilst there I talked to a large group of Japanese Christians, armed with cameras, genuflecting and praying – obviously most impressed with, and much enjoying, what they were experiencing. I had a word with the vicar, delightfully named Andrew Nutter, and presented him with a small china bowl decorated with a coloured image of Salisbury Cathedral.

On reflection I believe both the Dean and Chapter's decision in 1887 to allow the font to go off to Australia and to replace its Victorian successor in 2008 with that highly original modern font, designed by William Pye, to be brilliantly successful decisions.

The following quotation, amended slightly by the author of this book, may have some relevance:

> *'On this font which is in God's temple*
> *Rowan gently spilled the oil of might,*
> *That the dreams, which stirred in Jacob*
> *During the watches of the night,*
> *May be found in those his people*
> *Newly made Holy in God's sight'*

Appendix IV

The Mitre. Its Origin. The Changing Shape of Western Christian Mitres. Church of England Practice. The Mitre Elsewhere. A Postscript.

Its Origin

The Episcopal mitre derives from the early Asian, Greek and Latin word mitra, meaning turban; and, according to *Brewer's Dictionary of Phrase and Fable*, came to symbolise the cloven tongues of fire that descended on the Apostles on the day of Pentecost (Acts II: 1-12).

The Catholic Encyclopaedia notes that the pontifical mitre is of Roman origin derived from the non-liturgical head-covering (the camelaucum) of the Pope, which was worn as early as the beginning of the 8th century by Pope Constantine I: and also appears on the coins of Popes Sergius III (904-11) and Benedict VII (974-83). Successive Popes began to wear the mitre during the 10th century.

Roman Cardinals had the right to wear the mitre towards the end of the 11th century. The first authentic granting of the mitre to an Abbot dates from 1063 and soon even secular princes were granted permission to wear the mitre as a mark of distinction, (for example, Peter of Aragon was granted this privilege by Pope Innocent III (d. 1216). By about 1100-50 the custom of wearing the mitre had become general among bishops.

In the Catholic Church the right to wear the mitre is confined by Canon Law to bishops and to abbots as it appears in the ceremony of consecration of a bishop and blessing of an abbot. Cardinals are now normally supposed to be bishops (since the time of Pope John XXIII), but even cardinals, who are not bishops and who have been given special permission by the Pope to decline consecration as bishops, may wear the mitre. Other prelates have been granted the use of the mitre by special permission.

In its modern form in Western Christianity the mitre is a tall folding cap consisting of two similar parts (the front and back) rising to a peak and sewn together at the sides. Two short lappets – tails – hang down from the back.

The Changing Shape of Western Christian Mitres

The mitre shape changed dramatically between the 11th and the 20th centuries. In its earliest form the mitre was a simple cap of soft material, which ended above in a point, while around the lower edge there was often an ornamental band *(Diagram 1)*.

Towards 1100 the mitre began to develop a curved shape and became a skull cap *(Diagram 2)*. In more handsome mitres an ornamental band passed from front to back across the width which produced two prominent puffs in the upper part of the cap to left and right sides of the head *(Diagram 3)*.

In about 1125 the puffs began to develop into two horns *(Diagram 4)* which ended each in a point and was stuffed with parchment. This mitre grew into the next stage when the horns no longer sprouted from the temples of the wearer but from the forehead and the back of the head. Elaborate mitres of this kind had another ornamental band which went vertically over the middle of the horns *(Diagram 5)*.

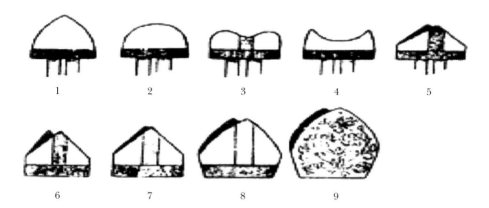

From the 14th century onwards, the mitre steadily rose in height until by the 17th century grew into a tower-like structure *(Diagrams 6 & 7)* and the sides of the mitre changed from vertical to diagonal *(Diagrams 8)* and many became heavily ornamented with silk, embroidery, goldwork and precious stones *(Diagram 9)*.

Church of England Practice

In Protestant England after the Reformation (c. 1539) the mitre fell out of use. But was revived in the late 19th century as a result of Oxford Movement influence and is now generally used by bishops of the Anglican Communion.

The Oxford Movement mentioned above (1837-45) was based in Oxford and led by John Keble (1792-1866), John Henry Newman (1801-96) and Edward Bouverie Pusey (1800-82). Its aim was to restore traditional Catholic teaching within the Church of England and, among other returns to the past, was the revival of ceremonial and the wearing of the mitre by bishops. At first the Movement met with much hostility particularly when Newman was received into the Roman Catholic Church in 1845. But later it maintained a following devoted to a closer relationship between the Anglican community and the Roman Catholic Church.

The Mitre Elsewhere

The Eastern Church (the Russian and Greek Orthodox Churches) and Judaism had their own versions of the mitre, its shape and its significance. These often developed into the most splendid and beautiful creations. There are many stunning examples to be found in Central and Eastern Europe museums and elsewhere in the Middle East. For those who wish to admire these, a visit to the Internet is recommended.

Postscript:
It is pleasant to recall that, not so long ago Bishop T, accompanied by his Suffragan Bishop M, agreed to rededicate the chapel of an English boarding school. The Bishop was seen to be a very tall lean man wearing a splendidly tall mitre; however, his Suffragan was observed to be comfortably small in stature and wore a neat little mitre. The two bishops processed side by side up the aisle. When the first hymn (A & M 573 – Mrs Alexander) was announced as 'All things bright and beautiful, all creatures great and small' it greatly stirred the youthful congregation and, later, was gleefully described in many letters home.

Index of Names (including The Wessex Factor – WF)

Bigod family of the 2nd Earl of Norfolk. Earl Marshal (1125-70) *pp.25, 101*

Biggs, John. Last Warden of De Vaux College when it was dissolved 1543 *p.117*

Bingham, Robert, Bishop of Salisbury. 1229-46 *pp.18, 80, 81, 99, 103, 119*

Blanche, of Castille, Queen of France, Wife of King Louis VIII (1188-1252) *pp.39, 43*

Bohun, Henry de. English landowner 13th C *pp.29, 33*

Bohun, Jocelin de. Bishop of Sarum (1142-84) d. 1186 *pp.17, 18*

Boniface, Marquis of Montferat, 4th Crusade Leader (c. 1202-04) and King of Thessalonika (1150-1207) *p.60*

Boniface of Savoy, Archbishop of Canterbury, hallowed Salisbury Cathedral 20. 9. 1258 *p.115*

Boyton, Thomas de. De Vaux College benefactor 1490 *p.116*

Brakespeare, Nicholas, Pope Adrian IV, the only English Pope *p.15*

Brewer, Lady Alice. Lady of the Manor of Worth Matravers and owner of purbeck stone mines 13th C *pp.92, 93*

Brian de Lisle, dissident English political faction, 13th C *p.44*

Brideoake, Ralph, Dean of Salisbury (1667-75) – his desk *pp.106, 107*

Buc, Walter. French mercenary leader during the Civil War (1215-17) *p.40*

Burgh, Hubert de, Earl of Kent. Regent of England and Chief Justiciar (1170-1243) *pp.37, 38, 41, 43- 47, 49, 50, 54-56, 76, 90*

Burgh, John de. Son of Hubert 13th C *p.54*

Burgh, Raymond de. Nephew of Hubert de Burgh 13th C *pp.45, 46*

Burnet, Gilbert. Bishop of Salisbury (1689-1715) *p.34*

Burton, Decimus, Architect. Restored Salisbury Cathedral mid 19th C *p.102*

Calixtus III, Pope. 15th C. Approved Canonisation of St Osmund *pp.12, 13*

Camville, Gerard de. Husband of Nicola de la Haie 13th C *p.42*

Camville, Richard de. Father of Idonea 13th C *pp.44, 64*

Canute, King of England (r. 1016-35). WF *p.21*

Careville, Robert. Cathedral Treasurer and De Vaux College Benefactor 13th C *p.116*

Cerdic, King of Wessex (r. 519-534) WF *p.7*

Charles I, King of England (r. 1623-49) *pp.37, 80, 107*

Charles II, King of England (r. 1649-restored 1660-1655) *pp.80, 107*

Charles III, Emperor of France 9th C *p.7*

Charworth, Sybil de, also called Sourches or Shaoures. See D'Evreux family tree

Chester, Earl of. Dissident English faction, 13th C *p.44*

Chetwood, Knightly, the King's Protestant Chaplain *p.83*

Christina, widow of William Manderville, Earl of Essex. She married Raymond de Burgh 12th C *p.45*

D'Evreux, Countess Ela daughter of Earl William D'Evreux. She m. 3rd Earl of Salisbury.
    12th C. See also separate entry under Longespée Ela, and the Longespée Family Tree

Fakhr ad Din. Co-Regent of Egypt 13th C *p.66*

Fawkes de Breaute, Royalist Leader in Civil War. Later dissident Leader of English faction
    1223 *pp.42, 44*

Ferrand, Count of Flanders. King John's Imperial Ally in France (1185-1233) *pp.31, 32*

Fitzosbern, Earl William (c. 1020-71). On his death the Earldom went into obeyance WF

Fort, Alexander. 17th C woodcarver *p.106*. See also illustration

Frederick II, Emperor of Germany, 5th Crusade Leader (1218-21) *p.60*

From Viking to Crusader, Scandinavians in Europe 800-1200 *p.7*

Gant, Gilbert de, a Leader of the rebel army at Lincoln in 1217 *p.42*

Geoffrey IV, The Handsome 9th Count of Anjou (1113-51), father of King Henry II Plantagent
    pp.23-25

Gerald, of Wales. Chronicler 13th C *p.31*

Gilbert de Clare, Earl of Gloucester c. 13th C *p.101*

Gifford, William. Emperor Matilda's Chancellor *p.51*

Giles de Bridport. Bishop of Salisbury 1257-63 *pp 11, 13, 15, 100, 114, 115, 119*

Gloucester, Earl Robert of. Besieged and burned the town of Wilton during the Anarchy 1143
    p.25

Godwin. Powerful Earl of Wessex (1001-53) WF

Goscelin, Monk of Wilton Abbey (c. 1046-1110) *p.22*

Gregorious IX, Pope. Papacy 1227-41 *pp.60, 114*

Guthrum, Scandinavian King of East Anglia (9th C) WF

Guy, King of Jerusalem 12th C during 2nd Crusade 1147-49 p.51

Hadrian, Abbot. North African Prelate 6th C *p.14*

Hahn, Kurt. 20th C International Educationalist. (Round Square Conference of Schools) *p.28*

Harding, Master William BCL. Fellow of De Vaux College Salisbury. Cathedral Chapter
    Clerk Son William was a Fellow of De Vaux College in 1470 *p.116*

Hardy, Thomas (1840-1928), Poet to whom the Revival of the name Wessex is due. WF

Harold, King of England (killed 1066 during Battle of Hastings). WF

Haie, Baron de la. Hereditary Castellan of Lincoln Castle, father of the intrepid Nicola
    pp.42, 44

Haie, Dame Nicola de la. Hereditary Castellan of Lincoln Castle 1215-17 Sheriff of Lincoln.
    Wife of Gerard de Camville *pp.42, 44, 56*

Harris, J. Pre-1715. Artist (see illustration *p.94*)

Addendum

The Berengar family lived in Provence, France in the 13th C and are of great interest and are worth noting. It all started when Count Ramon Berengar V (1195-1245) of Provence married Beatrice of Savoy, daughter of Thomas 1st, said to have been the most beautiful lady in the world (well, Matthew Paris thought the world of her as much for her beauty as for her brains, her political acumen and her selection of a powerful and popular husband). The marriage survived the severe shock of having two stillborn sons; but was blessed later with the welcome arrive of four strong-willed daughters who each married a European King.

We have also met Beatrice eldest daughter, Margaret Queen of France and her husband King Louis 1X (St Louis) and know of her amazing bravery during the 7th Crusade especially after the Battle of Mansourah in Egypt. What a stunner she was!

The next sister, Eleanor of Provence married King Henry 111 of England and accompanied her husband as chief guests at the hallowing of Salisbury Cathedral in 1258. The next sister Sanchia married Prince Richard of Cornwall who for a time was King of Germany. The last of the sisters, Beatrice married Charles 1 King of Sicily. All three sisters had exciting and worthwhile lives in a changing world; but, sadly, Sanchia and Beatrice died in their 34th year of age.

List of People and Resources

Author's Note

The Medieval Chroniclers of the Monastic School of St Alban's Abbey, Hertfordshire and in other Abbeys in England and France were highly respected in their time and especially during the period 1189-1259. Their work has been translated from Latin, French and Anglo-Norman into English over the centuries. One of the most interesting of these references has been the L'Histoire de Guillaume Le Marechal, the verse biography of William Marshal The Earl of Pembroke c. 1146-1219. It was written shortly after his death at the request of his son and is composed of 19,214 lines written in the Anglo-Norman language of the day. It describes in detail the major part of the Earl's life. It is based on the surviving account of his life by his Squire John D'Erlay and dates to the mid-13th century. The document is now in the Pierrepoint Morgan Library in New York. It was published in English by Paul Meyer in three volumes from 1891-1901.

The characters who appear on the front cover of this book include the following:

Bishop Richard Poore, Bishop Innocent III (younger and older), King John, the 2nd Earl of Pembroke (Marshal family), Earl William Longespée, Archbishop Stephen Langton and Bishop Saint Osmund.

Longespée Family Tree

(Abridged)

THE ROYAL HOUSE OF ANJOU

PLANTAGENET

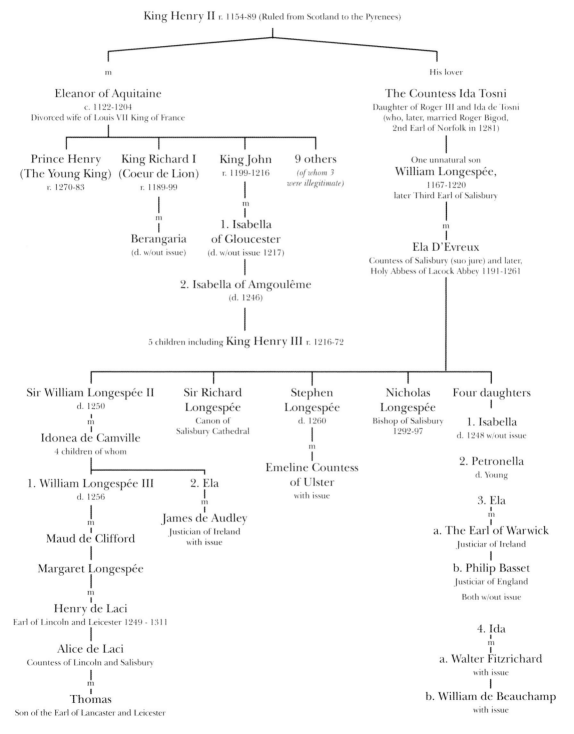

King Henry II r. 1154-89 (Ruled from Scotland to the Pyrenees)

m

His lover

Eleanor of Aquitaine
c. 1122-1204
Divorced wife of Louis VII King of France

The Countess Ida Tosni
Daughter of Roger III and Ida de Tosni
(who, later, married Roger Bigod,
2nd Earl of Norfolk in 1281)

Prince Henry
(The Young King)
r. 1270-83

King Richard I
(Coeur de Lion)
r. 1189-99

King John
r. 1199-1216

9 others
(of whom 3
were illegitimate)

One unnatural son
William Longespée,
1167-1220
later Third Earl of Salisbury

m

Berangaria
(d. w/out issue)

**1. Isabella
of Gloucester**
(d. w/out issue 1217)

m

Ela D'Evreux
Countess of Salisbury (suo jure) and later,
Holy Abbess of Lacock Abbey 1191-1261

2. Isabella of Amgoulême
(d. 1246)

5 children including **King Henry III** r. 1216-72

Sir William Longespée II
d. 1250

m

Idonea de Camville
4 children of whom

**Sir Richard
Longespée**
Canon of
Salisbury Cathedral

**Stephen
Longespée**
d. 1260

m

**Emeline Countess
of Ulster**
with issue

**Nicholas
Longespée**
Bishop of Salisbury
1292-97

Four daughters

1. Isabella
d. 1248 w/out issue

1. William Longespée III
d. 1256

m

Maud de Clifford

Margaret Longespée

m

Henry de Laci
Earl of Lincoln and Leicester 1249 - 1311

Alice de Laci
Countess of Lincoln and Salisbury

m

Thomas
Son of the Earl of Lancaster and Leicester

2. Ela

m

James de Audley
Justician of Ireland
with issue

2. Petronella
d. Young

3. Ela

m

a. The Earl of Warwick
Justiciar of Ireland

b. Philip Basset
Justiciar of England

Both w/out issue

4. Ida

m

a. Walter Fitzrichard
with issue

b. William de Beauchamp
with issue

D'Evreux Family Tree

(Abridged)

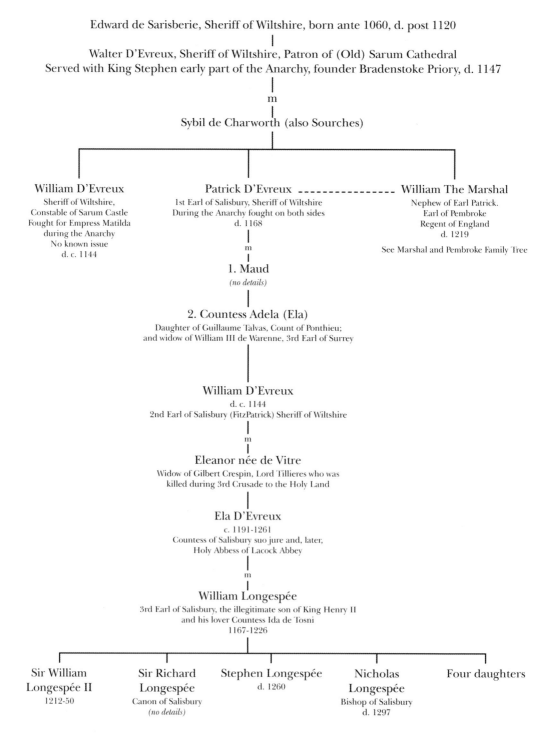

Edward de Sarisberie, Sheriff of Wiltshire, born ante 1060, d. post 1120

Walter D'Evreux, Sheriff of Wiltshire, Patron of (Old) Sarum Cathedral
Served with King Stephen early part of the Anarchy, founder Bradenstoke Priory, d. 1147

m

Sybil de Charworth (also Sourches)

William D'Evreux
Sheriff of Wiltshire,
Constable of Sarum Castle
Fought for Empress Matilda
during the Anarchy
No known issue
d. c. 1144

Patrick D'Evreux ------------- **William The Marshal**
1st Earl of Salisbury, Sheriff of Wiltshire
During the Anarchy fought on both sides
d. 1168

Nephew of Earl Patrick.
Earl of Pembroke
Regent of England
d. 1219

See Marshal and Pembroke Family Tree

m

1. Maud
(no details)

2. Countess Adela (Ela)
Daughter of Guillaume Talvas, Count of Ponthieu;
and widow of William III de Warenne, 3rd Earl of Surrey

William D'Evreux
d. c. 1144
2nd Earl of Salisbury (FitzPatrick) Sheriff of Wiltshire

m

Eleanor née de Vitre
Widow of Gilbert Crespin, Lord Tillieres who was
killed during 3rd Crusade to the Holy Land

Ela D'Evreux
c. 1191-1261
Countess of Salisbury suo jure and, later,
Holy Abbess of Lacock Abbey

m

William Longespée
3rd Earl of Salisbury, the illegitimate son of King Henry II
and his lover Countess Ida de Tosni
1167-1226

Sir William Longespée II
1212-50

Sir Richard Longespée
Canon of Salisbury
(no details)

Stephen Longespée
d. 1260

Nicholas Longespée
Bishop of Salisbury
d. 1297

Four daughters

See also Longespée Family Tree
(Abridged)

The Family Trees of the D'Evreux and Marshal Families (including the Earldom of Pembroke, Second Creation)

(Abridged)

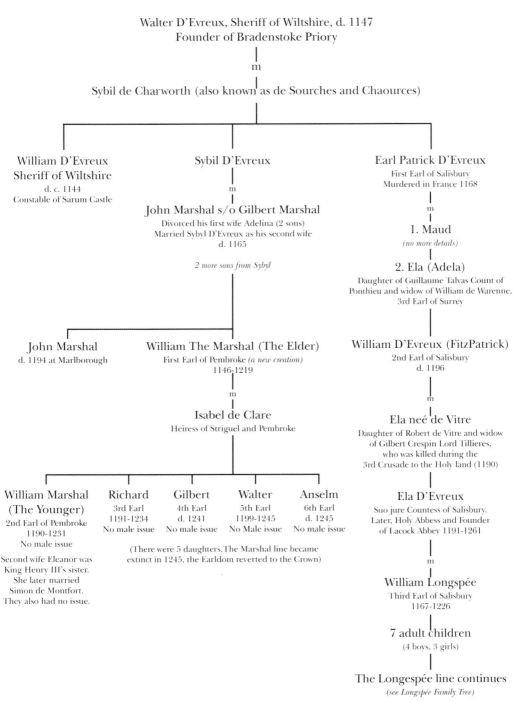

Edward D'Evreux, Sheriff of Wiltshire (de Sarisberie), born before 1060

Walter D'Evreux, Sheriff of Wiltshire, d. 1147
Founder of Bradenstoke Priory

m

Sybil de Charworth (also known as de Sources and Chaources)

William D'Evreux
Sheriff of Wiltshire
d. c. 1144
Constable of Sarum Castle

Sybil D'Evreux

m

John Marshal s/o Gilbert Marshal
Divorced his first wife Adelina (2 sons)
Married Sybyl D'Evreux as his second wife
d. 1165

2 more sons from Sybil

Earl Patrick D'Evreux
First Earl of Salisbury
Murdered in France 1168

m

1. Maud
(no more details)

2. Ela (Adela)
Daughter of Guillaume Talvas Count of
Ponthieu and widow of William de Warenne,
3rd Earl of Surrey

John Marshal
d. 1194 at Marlborough

William The Marshal (The Elder)
First Earl of Pembroke *(a new creation)*
1146-1219

m

Isabel de Clare
Heiress of Striguel and Pembroke

William D'Evreux (FitzPatrick)
2nd Earl of Salisbury
d. 1196

m

Ela neé de Vitre
Daughter of Robert de Vitre and widow
of Gilbert Crespin Lord Tillieres,
who was killed during the
3rd Crusade to the Holy land (1190)

William Marshal
(The Younger)
2nd Earl of Pembroke
1190-1231
No male issue

Second wife Eleanor was
King Henry III's sister.
She later married
Simon de Montfort.
They also had no issue.

Richard
3rd Earl
1191-1234
No male issue

Gilbert
4th Earl
d. 1241
No male issue

Walter
5th Earl
1199-1245
No Male issue

Anselm
6th Earl
d. 1245
No male issue

(There were 5 daughters. The Marshal line became
extinct in 1245, the Earldom reverted to the Crown)

Ela D'Evreux
Suo jure Countess of Salisbury.
Later, Holy Abbess and Founder
of Lacock Abbey 1191-1261

m

William Longspée
Third Earl of Salisbury
1167-1226

7 adult children
(4 boys, 3 girls)

The Longespée line continues
(see Longspée Family Tree)

145